Thomas Cook

BOSTON & NEW ENGLAND

BY

ROBERT HOLMES

Produced by

Thomas Cook Publishing

Written by Robert Holmes
Updated by Lura Seavey and Barbara Rogers
Original photography by Stillman D Rogers
Original design by Laburnum Technologies Pvt Ltd

Editing and page layout by Cambridge Publishing
Management Ltd, Unit 2, Burr Elm Court,
Caldecote CB3 7NU
Series Editor: Karen Beaulah

Published by Thomas Cook Publishing
A division of Thomas Cook Tour Operations Ltd

PO Box 227, The Thomas Cook Business Park,
Units 15–16, Coningsby Road,
Peterborough PE3 8SB, United Kingdom
E-mail: books@thomascook.com
www.thomascookpublishing.com
Tel: +44 (0) 1733 416477

ISBN-13: 978-1-84157-595-7
ISBN-10: 1-84157-595-X

Text © 2006 Thomas Cook Publishing
Maps © 2006 Thomas Cook Publishing
Subway map © 2006 Communicarta Ltd
First edition © 2002 Thomas Cook Publishing
Second edition © 2006 Thomas Cook Publishing

Project Editor: Linda Bass
Production/DTP Editor: Steven Collins

Printed and bound in Spain by: Grafo Industrias Gráficas, Basauri.

Cover design by: Liz Lyons Design, Oxford
Front cover credits: Left © Culliganphotos/Alamy; centre © Ezra Shaw/Getty; right © Demetrio
Carrasco/Alamy
Back cover credits: Left © David Lyons/Alamy; right © Ace Stock/Alamy

C o n t e n t s

KEY TO MAPS

✈ Airport

🚇 Subway

⭐ Start of walk/tour

ℹ️ Information

112 93   Road number

‑ ‑ ‑ Ferry route

1260m
▲   Mountain

Introduction

It may be called New England, but by American standards it is anything but new. Boston was founded 30 years before Charles II ascended to the British throne. Harvard University had been in existence for almost 20 years before Oliver Cromwell became Lord Protector. This is one of the few areas of the United States steeped in history on a European scale. It is the birthplace of the present-day United States of America, and the spiritual home of the American Revolution.

Brilliant foliage on a New Hampshire Pond

New England comprises the six north-eastern states of the United States: Massachusetts, Connecticut, Vermont, New Hampshire, Maine and tiny Rhode Island. The city of Boston has always been regarded as the region's capital.

New England

Throughout its history, New England has always exerted an influence far greater than its size. Both Yale and Harvard are here, along with many equally prestigious seats of academia. It is home to 7.5 per cent of the nation's graduate schools, and Greater Boston alone has 65 colleges and universities.

Boston has had many of the nation's 'firsts' – among them the first public library, public park, children's museum and computer museum. It is a world leader in the high-technology computer industry, rivalling California's Silicon Valley, and Hartford, Connecticut, has long been the centre of the nation's insurance industry.

In complete contrast, the New England countryside has come to epitomise rural America. Connecticut, Rhode Island and Massachusetts are more affluent and punctuated with major urban centres, while thinly populated Vermont, New Hampshire and Maine are genuinely rural and agricultural, even relatively poor in parts. Images of white steepled churches peeping through brilliant autumn foliage, and misty fishing harbours sheltering on a rocky coastline, are as much a part of the idealised American iconography as the evocative, richly detailed paintings of Norman Rockwell, himself a New Englander (*see* Stockbridge, *p92*).

This is one of the most cultural corners of America. Publishing, encouraged by the proximity of so much intellectual activity, has always thrived in the area. Many great literary figures have made their homes here, from Henry David Thoreau and Harriet Beecher Stowe, to Henry Wadsworth Longfellow and Robert Frost. The museums and art galleries of Boston are world-class in both scope and importance, and the Boston Symphony is as fine an orchestra as you will find anywhere.

Whatever your interests – from nature to culture, tradition to technology – you can find them in New England.

Boston's exciting landscape

Land and People

If geography shapes human character, then New Englanders owe their formidable spirit and stubborn Yankee disposition to a landscape that is at once beautiful and harsh, generous and unforgiving. Scoured by glaciers, pounded by ocean waves and carved by an extensive system of rivers and streams, New England – the most compact region in the United States – offers a diverse landscape that seems to change with every mountain valley and sandy coastline.

Fit for a feast: Atlantic lobster

The Appalachians, America's oldest mountain range, form the backbone of New England. Stretching 1,600 miles from the St Lawrence Valley in Canada to Alabama, the range branches off into two distinct New England mountain chains. The Green Mountains form a north–south ridge that runs through the centre of the state of Vermont. Mount Mansfield, Vermont's tallest peak, and nearby Camels Hump are favourites among Green Mountain hikers. The mountain range extends south into Massachusetts, where it is better known as the Berkshire Hills.

Sculpted by receding glaciers, the spectacular White Mountains rise like sentries on the New Hampshire landscape. At 6,288 feet, Mount Washington, the highest point in the northeastern United States, is the jewel of the White Mountains. With its towering peaks, the Mount Washington Valley region inspired the White Mountains School of Art, a group of 19th-century landscape painters who brought fame to the region. Continuing

north and east, the mountain chain pushes into Maine. Heading southeast, the only major mountain is Mount Monadnock, a majestic, isolated peak often climbed by Henry David Thoreau.

Between these mighty mountain ranges lies the Connecticut River Valley, an area of a hundred lakes, gentle hills and pristine colonial villages. Stretching 400 miles, the valley follows the course of the Connecticut River, which forms the border between Vermont and New Hampshire and divides the New England region in half.

As mountains give way to rolling hills, New England's character gives way to a coastline that is both harsh and inviting. The jagged and irregular Maine coast has an untamed feel. It was formed by retreating glaciers 11,000 years ago, that left behind a bedrock of sandstone, limestone and shale. Here, peninsulas jut into the icy North Atlantic waters, and rocky islands with windswept pines provide a rugged retreat.

New England's most famous coastline, however, is the expanse of superb sand beaches that form the landscape of Cape Cod and the islands of Nantucket and Martha's Vineyard. These areas were formed some 100,000 years ago as a glacier pulled away, leaving behind clay, sand and rocky debris. Most of the glacial moraine formed Cape Cod, with the outermost protrusions forming the islands. Time, tides and weather have created a masterpiece along the coast: great rolling dunes, miles of beaches, and an austere plant life that ekes out an existence on the edge of the continent.

The People

The original Indian tribes of New England – the Penobscot, Passamaquoddy, Wampanoag and Mashpee – have all but disappeared. As happened all over America, they were wiped out either by warfare, or by disease introduced by the settlers. The final blow was a 'war' started by an Indian named Philip. Concerned about the growing dominance of the whites, he persuaded several tribes to band together to fight the English. 'King Philip', as the Colonists called him, was betrayed and King Philip's War broke out in 1675. By the time he was killed in 1676, the Indian population had been virtually exterminated. The few Native Americans (the correct name for these original inhabitants that remain today) live on reservations in Maine, Cape Cod and Martha's Vineyard.

Until the mid-1800s, most of the population were descendants of the British Puritans. These Yankees were hard-working and adaptable. Their renowned ingenuity gave New England a tremendous boost during the

Industrial Revolution. Several inventions, such as the cotton gin, established New England as the industrial centre of the nation. The great Irish potato famine of 1845 resulted in an enormous influx of Irish immigrants attracted by the wealth of New England and the availability of jobs. Lithuanians, Poles, Germans and Russian Jews followed. The Italians came in the 1870s and, later, French Canadians – all in search of work.

In Boston, the black community that lived in the North End was replaced by the Irish, then by the Jews, and finally by the Italians, who remain there to this day. The blacks moved to Beacon Hill before finally settling in the larger cities of southern New England. Beacon Hill became, and still is, a quarter for the social aristocracy, nicknamed the 'Boston Brahmins'. These wealthy, white Anglo-Saxons constitute America's nearest equivalent to the British upper class.

Franconia Notch

Dartmouth College

History

The first settlers were the Algonquin Indians, who lived by hunting, fishing and raising basic crops. By the 17th century their population was already in sharp decline through disease and tribal warfare.

1602	Cape Cod is named by Explorer Bartholomew Gosnold.
1613	Jesuits establish a mission on Mount Desert Island, off the coast of Maine.
1614	The term 'New England' is used for the first time in Captain John Smith's *A Description of New England*. Smith sails into the Boston area and names the Charles River. Adrian Block, a Dutch navigator, names Block Island off the coast of Rhode Island.
1620	Plymouth Colony, one of the first permanent English settlements, is established by Pilgrims arriving on the *Mayflower*.
1626	Roger Conant and a group of settlers establish the Puritan colony of Salem.
1630	Boston is founded under the leadership of Puritan John Winthrop.

1634	Boston Common is purchased.
1636	Harvard College is founded. Roger Williams establishes Providence, Rhode Island.
1662	A royal charter unites the colonies of New Haven and Connecticut.
1770	On 5 March the Boston Massacre occurs: five colonists are killed by British bullets outside the Old State House.
1773	On 16 December the Boston Tea Party takes place: 342 chests of tea are tossed into Boston Harbor by colonists dressed as Indians.
1775	The start of the American Revolution. **18 April** The rides of Paul Revere and William Dawes. **19 April** Battles of Concord and Lexington. **17 June** Battle of

	Bunker Hill. **3 July** George Washington takes command of the Continental Army on Cambridge Common.
1776	The British evacuate Boston in March. **4 July** Declaration of Independence.
1777	The Battle of Bennington, Vermont. Vermont is declared an independent republic.
1783	End of the American Revolution. Britain accepts independence.
1820	Maine becomes the 23rd state of the Union.
1821	Horace Mann opens America's first free public school.
1826	Mayor Josiah Quincy starts construction of Quincy Market.
1845	Irish fleeing the potato famine arrive in Boston.
1851	Harriet Beecher Stowe starts work on her novel *Uncle Tom's Cabin* in Hartford, Connecticut.
1852	The first public library in America opens in Boston.

1872	The Great Fire destroys 770 buildings over 65 acres in the heart of the downtown area.
1897	The first underground railway system in America opens under Boston Common at Park Street.
1910	John F Fitzgerald, the grandfather of John F Kennedy, is elected mayor of Boston.
1954	The world's first atomic submarine, the *Nautilus*, is constructed at Groton, Connecticut.
1960	Kennedy casts his ballot in the Old West Church a few hours before being elected President.
1976	Quincy Market reopens after extensive restoration.
1980	Boston celebrates its 350th anniversary.
1996	The 100th Boston Marathon takes place.
2001	The Union Oyster House, America's oldest restaurant, celebrates 175 years.
2004	The Boston Red Sox win baseball's World Series, ending an 86-year 'curse'.

Governance

The birthplace of the American Revolution, New England has always been a free-thinking region where politics are a regular topic of conversation. This unfettered state of mind has created a brand of political thinking that holds steady in shifting political winds and exerts a powerful influence. While the rest of the country jumps on the latest bandwagon, little New England continues to declare its independence. In doing so, it reminds its fellow Americans of the core values that form the foundation of American democracy. The following is a brief look at the political history of New England, state by state.

Connecticut

Connecticut will always have a place in political history as the state where the world's first written constitution was introduced. In recent years, both in local and national politics, this has been a Democratic stronghold, although in presidential elections, the electorate has tended to favour Republicans.

In the 1990s the state elected former Republican Congressman and Senator Lowell Weicker, Jr. Governor as an independent. Democrats have since returned to top offices. In 2004 Senator Joseph Lieberman rose to national prominence as the Democrat nominee for Vice President. He and Senator Christopher Dodd are leaders for progressive causes in the Senate.

Maine

Maine's rocky, deeply indented coast coincides with the state's independent political mind. Numerous independents have been elected Governor. Former Senator George Mitchell later brokered peace in Ireland after serving as Senate majority leader. Former President Bush still maintains a summer home at Kennebunkport, which his son, the present President Bush, occasionally visits.

Massachusetts

Flash point of the American Revolution, the

GOVERNING BOSTON

The city of Boston is governed by a mayor, elected for a four-year term, and a city council – but it wasn't always so. Originally, Boston was a self-governing Puritan community established and run by the Massachusetts Bay Company. When the company lost its influence with the British throne, it lost its charter and Boston became part of the royal Province of Massachusetts ruled by a Colonial governor until the American Revolution.

Boston was the hotbed of Revolutionary fervour. Sam Adams and Paul Revere, the Old North Church and the Boston Tea Party are all important to the history – and mythology – of the American Revolution. The traditional town meeting, the instrument of New England democracy, soon became unwieldy. In 1822 the state granted Boston a city charter, the basis of the city's modern government.

state is still known as the home of political liberalism. Its political heritage gave it such colourful leaders as John Quincy and Samuel Adams, Mayor James Curley, the nationally influential Kennedy family, and most recently the Democrat Party Presidential nominee, Senator John Kerry. The large number of universities in the Boston area creates an intellectual ferment that often attaches itself to the solution of social and governmental problems both within the state and nationally.

New Hampshire
Small in size, the state is in many ways a microcosm of the country. Thought of as agricultural, it is actually heavily

State House, Boston

industrialised, with strong growth in technology fields. With no sales or income taxes, it attracts businesses and shoppers from neighbouring states. Its 'first-in-the-nation' Presidential Primary has made it the 'must win' state, exerting tremendous influence on the scope and direction of national political debate.

Rhode Island
Ever since the New Deal of the 1930s, Democrats have dominated politics in this, the nation's smallest state. Its Senators, notably the Pell family and Senator John Chaffee, have been powerful national leaders. Allegations of corruption weakened Democrat control over the last decade. It has no county government but is divided into 39 self-governing local communities.

Vermont
Long thought of as a staunch Republican stronghold, the state has for some time been fiercely independent and progressive. Its state leadership has been in the vanguard of solutions to issues such as universal child healthcare coverage, control of environmental degradation, progressive tax policies, gay rights and preservation of water and agricultural resources. Long-term and popular Governor Howard Dean rose to national prominence in the 2004 Presidential elections and went on to serve as Democrat National Party Chairman. Its Senators, Jim Jeffords and Patrick Leahy, and its lone Congressman, former Socialist Burlington Mayor (and now Independent) Bernard Sanders, are nationally known leaders.

It was a complete accident that the Pilgrims aboard the *Mayflower* landed where they did. The 102 colonists under the leadership of William Brewster had set sail from Plymouth, England, for the Virginia Colony at Jamestown, but they were blown off course. First sighting land at Cape Cod, they cruised the coast for a month until 21 December 1620 when, in search of a more hospitable environment, they crossed the bay to Plymouth. Here they established their famous settlement.

The first winter was so harsh that almost half the Pilgrims died. Friendly Indians came to the rescue with much-needed food, and in the autumn of 1621 Indian Chief Massasoit shared the original Thanksgiving feast with Governor William Bradford and the Pilgrims.

The Pilgrims were Puritans fleeing England in the wave of reform that was flowing through the Church. They had deeply held religious convictions, and were committed to the 'purification' of the Church of England. Persecuted for these beliefs, they went in search of new lands where they could have the freedom to follow their ideals. Many more followed the *Mayflower* Pilgrims, and by 1630 the Massachusetts Bay Colony had been founded. By 1636 there were over 12,000 Puritans in settlements along the coast, and in New Hampshire and Connecticut. The need for Puritan clergy resulted in

the establishment of Harvard College to train future ministers. The downfall of the Puritans was their total lack of tolerance for the beliefs of others. The Salem witch trials were a typical example of their fanaticism, but they

THANKSGIVING

Celebrated on the fourth Thursday of November, Thanksgiving is a time for gathering with family and close friends to share the bounty of the harvest (these days, often timed to fit in with televised football games). Although food traditions vary around the country, the meal typically centres on turkey, cranberry sauce, cornbread and pumpkin pie – all originally from New England, but adopted by Americans everywhere. The meal may resemble Christmas, but the holiday itself has a patriotic underpinning that sets it quite apart from December's festivities.

Facing page: Statue of Roger Conant, founder of Salem; right: the Salem Witch Museum; below: House of the Seven Gables, Salem

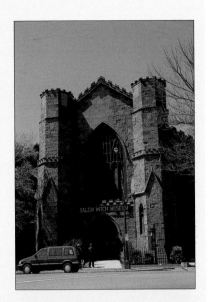

also persecuted other religious groups, such as the Quakers, Baptists and Jews.

Roger Williams, who disagreed with this extreme attitude, was banished from the colony for his 'dangerous views'. He founded Rhode Island, which became the first state to grant complete religious freedom. Other states soon followed the same course and, long before the American Revolution, Puritanism had become a thing of the past. So precious was the principle of religious freedom that it was enshrined in the Constitution's Bill of Rights.

Culture

New England is in many ways the most European of the American regions. It has history, the architecture is usually of European derivation, and the people tend to have a European temperament.

Proud Traditionalists

New Englanders tend to be more reserved than the average American and more in love with tradition. You will find in Boston America's closest equivalent to the British class system. For a start, there is a distinct Boston accent, which many Americans consider 'refined'. Then there are the 'Boston Brahmins', a name coined by Oliver Wendell Holmes back in the 19th century. These were originally the wealthy merchants of the city, almost always descendants of the early Puritan settlers. They were well-educated (usually at Harvard), well-read, well-travelled and very conservative. As the old saying goes, 'The Lowells talk only to the Cabots, and the Cabots talk only to God.'

This attitude persists to this day and can be encountered in institutions like the Boston Athenaeum.

The Daughters of the American Revolution (DAR) is typical of the organisations that still have a very loyal and active membership. Exclusive men's clubs are also a Boston tradition, though times are changing a little, and most of them now have to admit women to membership.

Today, it is fair to say that only a tiny minority

Antique store, Essex

cling to the old elitist attitude. One reason for this is that, as other ethnic groups came over to the New World, the population became much more diverse. The 'proper Bostonian' is alive and well but rarely found outside of Boston and its wealthy western suburbs.

Other areas of New England are much more relaxed and informal. The whole of the northern area, including the states of Vermont, New Hampshire and Maine, is very rural and, while the people have an easy-going attitude to life, they remain fiercely independent.

Quincy Market, a top tourist magnet

Festivals and Events

JANUARY
Massachusetts
Chinese New Year, Boston
(*sometimes February*).
Boston Cooks, Boston.
Vermont
Winter Carnival, Stowe.

FEBRUARY
Massachusetts
Black History Month,
Boston.
Winter Festival, Boston.
New Hampshire
Dartmouth Winter
Carnival, Hanover.

MARCH
Massachusetts
Boston Massacre
Ceremony, Boston.
New England Spring
Garden and Flower Show,
Boston.
St Patrick's Day, Boston
and Providence.

APRIL
Maine
Fisherman's Festival,
Boothbay Harbour.
Massachusetts
Boston Marathon, Boston.
Patriot's Day, Lexington.
New Hampshire
5-College Book Sale,
Hanover.
Vermont
Maple Sugar Festival,
St Johnsbury.

State Maple Festival,
St Albans.

MAY
Connecticut
Lobster Festival, Mystic
Seaport.
New England Fiddle
Contest, Hartford.
Maine
Maine State Parade,
Lewiston.
Massachusetts
Beacon Hill Hidden
Garden Tour, Boston.
Harvard Square May Fair,
Cambridge.
Street Performers Festival,
Boston.
New Hampshire
Sheep and Wool Festival,
New Boston.

JUNE
Massachusetts
Ancient and Honorable
Artillery Company Parade,
Boston.
Boston Globe Jazz Festival,
Boston.
Bunker Hill Day, Boston.
Cambridge River Festival,
Cambridge.
Dragon Boat Festival,
Boston.
Harborlights Music
Festival, Boston
(*June to September*).
Garden Month, Old
Sturbridge Village.

BEST FESTIVALS

Music lovers should
not miss the
summer Tanglewood
Music Festival when the
Boston Philharmonic
Orchestra plays the
Berkshire Hills.

In Boston, the Boston
Pops Orchestra starts its
traditional concerts in the
Shell on 4 July. Also in
Boston, on 4 July, is
Harborfest, a festival
which occurs throughout
the city with several
recreations of New
England's colonial past.

The Boston Marathon,
one of the nation's most
impressive athletic events,
takes place on the third
Monday of April. In late
June, Block Island, Rhode
Island, is home to Race
Week for hundreds of
sailing boats.

In late October,
Vermont's Northeast
Kingdom stages a week-
long Fall Foliage Festival
with country fairs in many
of the region's villages.

At various times
throughout the summer,
Providence's Waterplace
Park celebrates Waterfire
with river bonfires and
outdoor concerts.

New Hampshire
Blessing of the Fleet, Portsmouth.
Rhode Island
Festival of Historic Homes, Providence.
Race Week, Block Island.

JULY
Connecticut
Ancient Fife and Drum Corps Parade
and Muster, Deep River.
New England Arts and Crafts Festival,
Milford.
Massachusetts
Fourth of July; Harborfest;
North End Festivals;
Pops Esplanade Concerts, Boston.
Tanglewood Music Festival, Lenox.
New Hampshire
Woodsmen's Festival, Berlin.
Rhode Island
Black Ships Festival, Newport.
Newport Music Festival, Newport.

AUGUST
Connecticut
Quinnehtukqut Rendezvous and
Native American Festival, Haddam.
Maine
Fryeburg Fair, Fryeburg.
Massachusetts
August Moon Festival, Boston.
Berkshire Crafts Fair, Great Barrington.
Caribbean Carnival Festival, Boston.
Faneuil Hall Marketplace Festival,
Boston.
New Hampshire
Craftsmen Fair, Sunapee.
Moose Festival, Colebrook.

SEPTEMBER
Maine
Common Ground Fair.

Massachusetts
Cranberry Festival, South Carver.
Gallops Island Cider Fest,
Boston.
New England's 'Big E' Fair, West
Springfield.
Rhode Island
International Sailboat Show,
Newport.
Jazz Festival, Newport.
Vermont
Dowsers Festival, Danville.

OCTOBER
Massachusetts
Columbus Day, Boston.
Harvest Weekend, Old Sturbridge
Village.
Head of the Charles Regatta,
Boston.
Music Festival, Worcester.
New Hampshire
Fall Foliage Festival, Warner.
Pumpkin Festival, Keene.
Vermont
Northeast Kingdom Foliage Festival,
Peacham, Groton.

NOVEMBER
Massachusetts
Thanksgiving Day Celebration,
Plymouth.
Veterans Day Parade, Boston.

DECEMBER
Massachusetts
Tea Party Re-enactment, Boston.
Rhode Island
Christmas in Newport, Newport.
New Hampshire
Candlelight Stroll, Strawbery Banke,
Portsmouth.

Impressions

Boston, the cosmopolitan capital of Massachusetts, is the most European of American cities. In spite of its population (Boston is the seventh largest city in the United States, with over 2 million inhabitants), it is quite compact, and is one of the very few American cities in which walking is a delight.

A shady walk down Charles Street

Driving

For most visitors the first contact comes after picking up a car at the airport, although in Boston itself a car is a definite handicap. At Boston's Logan Airport the city is so close that it is better to jump straight into a taxi or onto the convenient Silver Line T bus and head for the hotel. But as soon as you leave the city, a car will be a necessity. Public transport outside the cities is not very good, although you can get to some tourist regions (including the Maine coast) by train or bus. New England is a compact area and is both quick and easy to get around with a car. Driving is on the right, and although the city traffic may appear intimidating, no one goes very fast.

One disturbing aspect of travel is that people overtake on both sides. There is, theoretically, a fast lane, but it is not unheard of to find someone in it pottering along at 40mph. Fortunately, lane discipline is very good, but remember to keep your eyes open, and use your mirrors frequently.

Speed limits are 55 or 65mph on interstate highways with 55mph close to cities. Follow the clearly posted speed limit signs. Speeding tickets are very expensive, so take care. Patrol cars operate on all roads, and radar traps are frequently used in towns and cities. Drink-driving laws are extremely tough.

Parking

Looking for a parking space, particularly in city centres, can be like searching for the Holy Grail.

Charles Street MTA station

Busy traffic on Storrow Drive

Street parking is generally regulated by meters, with time limits ranging from 15 minutes to 4 hours. Almost all accept quarters (25-cent coins). The most expensive meters in major city centres cost $1 for 30 minutes.

If a meter is obviously out of order, the usual solution is to write 'Meter Broken' on a paper bag and place it over the meter, usually preventing a parking ticket.

Always read notices attached to meters and street signs. On major streets in cities, parking is often restricted at peak commuting times. The most common hours are 7–9am and 4–6pm, and during these periods you will not only get a hefty parking ticket, but also have your car towed away at considerable additional expense.

A wheelchair symbol indicates a zone exclusively reserved for disabled motorists. Do not park in these zones – they carry the highest parking penalty.

All streets without meters are available for parking unless otherwise posted, but remember to park in the direction of the traffic.

Parking is sometimes prohibited for a couple of hours one day of the week for street cleaning, so read the small print on street signs.

Boston subway

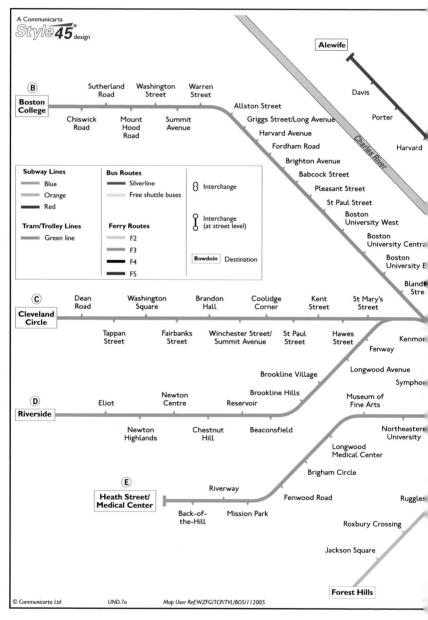

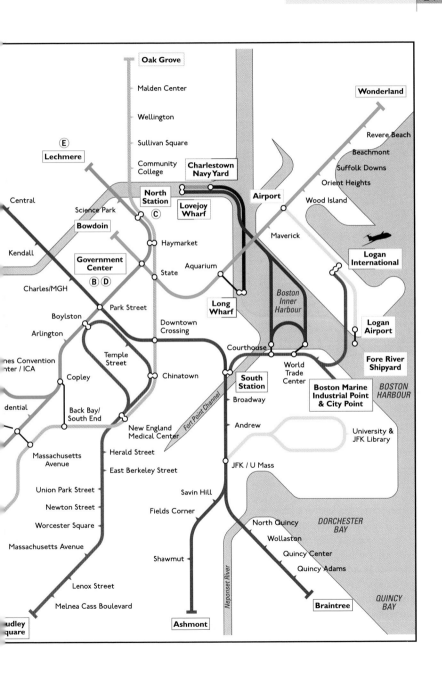

New Englanders love to trade at local farm stands

Services and Shops

Most visitors are impressed with the quality of service in New England. Restaurant staff are nearly always polite and efficient, and even the conventional send-off of 'Have a nice day' is more often meant than not. American restaurant servers expect tips. It is normal to leave 15 per cent of the total bill in restaurants, more if the service has been above average.

Service standards are generally high, and there is a strong work ethic. Shops are open late, and some never close (although in the more rural areas of New England there may only be one general store in the village, and it is unlikely to stay open late). Most major supermarkets are open until at least 10pm, and often until midnight. The 7–11 chain of convenience stores never closes at all, and they can be found open in most larger towns 365 days of the year. They stock a basic range of foodstuffs and also serve coffee and some fast foods. Even the big department stores open late at least one night a week, and all but the smallest shops are open on Sundays.

Sales are a way of life here, and most weeks one store or another will be having one. Filene's Basement in Boston is one permanent sale that has become a New England institution. The prices can sometimes be unbelievably low and, depending on foreign exchange rates, incredible bargains can be found. Local newspapers always carry advertisements with details.

Remember that if a state charges sales tax, it is always added to the marked price. Nothing is more frustrating than waiting in a long queue at the cash register to pay to find that the item you thought you had just enough money to buy has an additional 5 to 7 per cent added. The exact rate will depend on the state you are in (New Hampshire has no sales tax).

The Boston City Pass offers visitors free admission to participating museums. The passes can be bought at any one of their museums and are valid for one year. The museums include the Museum of Science, New England Aquarium, Skywalk Observatory, Harvard Museum of Natural History, John F Kennedy Library and Museum, and the Museum of Fine Arts, Boston.

Seafaring craftsmanship continues at the Wooden Boat School, Newport RI

Boston

Boston is a relatively compact city. Most of the major sights are within walking distance of each other, and the public transport system is excellent.

The Boston Visitor Pass offers free transport on the T buses, underground (subway) and inner harbour ferries. Available in 1-, 3- and 7-day units, they can be ordered online at *www.mbta.com*. You can begin using them at the airport.

The underground railway, the MBTA (popularly referred to as the T), covers the whole of the greater Boston area speedily, cleanly and safely. Even Logan Airport is close to downtown and can be quickly reached by subway.

In America, Boston is second only to San Francisco in popularity with tourists. An American travel magazine survey placed Boston as the seventh most popular city in the world, surpassed only by Paris, London, Rome, Vienna, Venice and San Francisco.

What accounts for such popularity? One reason, surely, is the tangible sense of history in Boston. It is in many ways the birthplace of the United States.

The city's museums and art galleries have world-class collections, and in Boston the visitor is offered everything, from the finest dining to shopping that ranges from bargains to ultimate chic.

Beyond all of this, Boston is the gateway to New England – a region of unique beauty and charm.

(For blue numbers, see Walk, pp46–7. For green numbers, see Walk, pp48–9. For orange numbers, see Walk, pp50–1. For yellow numbers, see Walk, pp52–3.)

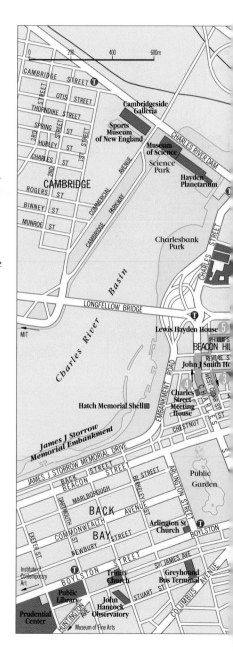

Boston City

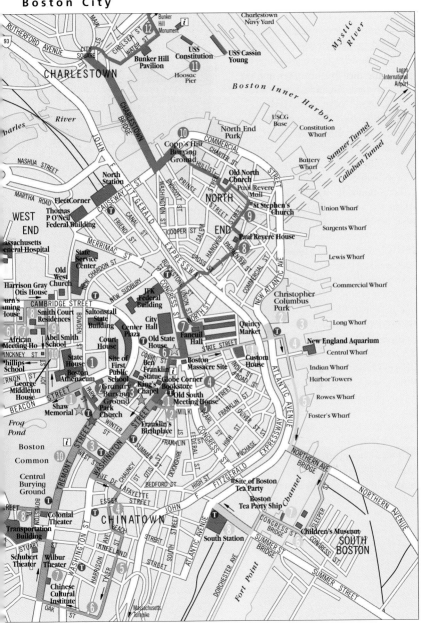

Alexander Graham Bell Museum Tour

In the heart of downtown Boston, in the building which locals still call the New England Telephone Building, is one of the smallest museums you will find anywhere. A dark, cupboard-like room, just off the entrance lobby, houses a detailed reconstruction of the attic where the first electrical transmission of speech over a wire marked the birth of the telephone on 3 June 1875.

The original building, occupied by Alexander Graham Bell – one of the most prolific inventors of the 19th century – was demolished in the late 1920s, but each piece of wood from the attic was removed, numbered and noted on precise plans, then reassembled in its present location in 1959.

The tour consists of a re-creation of Alexander Graham Bell's attic laboratory in his Boston home of 1875.
Verizon, 185 Franklin St, Boston 02107. Tel: (617) 743 4747.
http://boston.sidewalk.citysearch.com/ E/V/BOSMA/0017/87/12/cs1.html.
Open: Mon–Fri 8am–6pm. Free admission. South Station stop on the Red Line.

Arnold Arboretum

Out on Boston's Jamaica Plain, this 265-acre park forms a major link in the city's 'Emerald Necklace'. Established in 1872, it contains over 7,000 varieties of trees and plants from around the world. The self-guided walks are recommended (*maps from the Visitor Center*).
125 Arborway, Jamaica Plain. Tel: (617) 524 1718/524 1717 for blossom information. Open: daily sunrise–sunset.

Louisburg Square in Boston's Beacon Hill District is a genteel, residential area

Beacon Hill

Beacon Hill lies to the northwest of Boston Common and slopes down to the Charles River. The name was derived from the light used in 1634 to warn colonial settlers of danger. Now it is an exclusive residential area topped by the golden-domed State House. There is no more charming area in Boston than the Hill, and it has been a much sought-after address for over two centuries. The atmosphere is typically English, with red-brick mansions and narrow cobblestone streets – so English, in fact, that film companies often use the area as a location to represent old London.

A good introduction to Beacon Hill is the African-American Heritage Trail (*see pp48–9*), but there are some interesting detours.

Acorn Street, off West Cedar Street, is a picture-perfect, narrow cobblestone street, originally the home of servants to the nearby mansions, and perhaps the most photographed street in Boston, benefiting greatly from the ban on parking. Across Mount Vernon Street is exclusive **Louisburg Square** with its private central park. The 19th-century author, Louisa May Alcott (*Little Women*), lived at No. 10, and the square is still considered the most sophisticated address in Boston.

At 55 Mount Vernon Street, the **Nichols House Museum** is a good example of a 19th-century row (terraced) house. Rose Standish Nichols was a pioneer landscape architect and peace advocate, and the niece of sculptor Augustus Saint-Gaudens. The house is full of memorabilia, sculptures and antique furnishings. *Tel: (617) 227 6993 for opening times.*

Harrison Gray Otis was a larger-than-life developer who also became Mayor of Boston, and a member of the Senate. He had three houses built in Boston, all designed by his friend Charles Bulfinch. His second house, at 85 Mount Vernon Street, was one of the biggest on the Hill, but he soon moved on to 45 Beacon Street. Also worth noting here are the **Appleton-Parker Houses** at Nos 39–40. These two identical buildings were designed in the Greek Revival style for a pair of wealthy merchants. Number 39 witnessed the marriage of Fanny Appleton to Henry Wadsworth Longfellow in 1843. Notice the purple windowpanes. Shipments of glass sent from Hamburg to Boston between 1818 and 1824 contained magnesium, which turned the glass purple in the New England sunlight. These are some of the only authentic examples of Beacon Hill glass that remain.
T Station: Park St.

Boston's ever-changing waterfront

Boston Athenaeum

Visitors who respect its dignified and quiet atmosphere are welcomed at this bastion of Old Boston, founded in 1807. The 1849 building is a National Historic Landmark and is well worth visiting, especially if you reserve a space on their Tuesday or Thursday tours.

Architecturally, the interior is superb, with high, vaulted ceilings and dozens of marble busts in pillared archways. It was the home of Boston's first fine art gallery, and it still houses an impressive collection of paintings by such artists as John Singer Sargent and Gilbert Stuart. Visitors are allowed to tour the library, which includes the private collection of George Washington.

The leather-chaired Reading Room on the fifth floor is the most splendid in the Athenaeum. The Old Granary Burying Ground can be seen from the balcony. *101/2 Beacon St. Tel: (617) 227 0270. Open: Mon 9am–8pm, Tue–Fri 9am–5.30pm, Sat 9am–4pm. Tours: Tue & Thur. Closed: Jul–mid-Sept. Free admission. T station: Park St.*

Boston Common

In the very heart of Boston is a 50-acre parcel of land that has been a public park since 1634, making it the oldest in the country. Originally the land was used for grazing and militia training. Now it is an urban green swath for strolling, picnicking and – for children –

The Common's Frog Pond is a great wading pool for children

cavorting in the playground or splashing in the Frog Pond, which becomes a free skating rink in winter. Sadly, like urban parks everywhere, this is not a safe place to be at night.
T station: Park St and Boylston.

Boston Globe Tours
The *Boston Globe* is one of America's most respected daily newspapers, and free tours are offered to anyone wishing to see how a major newspaper works, including the printing presses (no children under nine years). The *Globe* building is not far from the JFK Library and Museum, and a combined visit avoids having to make two trips to this outpost in south Boston.
135 Morrissey Blvd, Dorchester.
Tel: (617) 929 2653. By appointment.
T station: JFK/U Mass. Free admission.

Boston Massacre Site
The site of the Boston Massacre – where five Patriots were killed by British troops in 1770 – is marked by a small ring of stones embedded in the pavement in State Street, just in front of the Old State House. It is very easy to miss in the midst of the surrounding modern commercial buildings.
T station: State.

Boston Public Library
America's finest talents were brought together to build the most magnificent library in the land – architects McKim, Mead and White, painters John Singer Sargent, Edwin Abbey and Puvis de Chavannes, and sculptors Bela Pratt, Augustus Saint-Gaudens and Daniel Chester French. On completion in 1895,

The Esplanade alongside the Charles River is a perfect place to stroll or relax

it admirably lived up to its name as a 'Palace for the People'. Although somewhat faded, it is still a fine example of lavish municipal architecture. Look for the murals by Sargent, and linger in the Italianate central courtyard.
666 Boylston St (at Dartmouth St).
Tel: (617) 536 5400. Open: Mon–Thur 9am–9pm, Fri & Sat 9am–5pm, Sun 1–5pm. Free tours on Fri & Sat 11am. Closed: Sun in summer.
T Station: Copley/Back Bay.

Boston Tea Party Ship
A replica of one of the three original two-masted Danish brigs sits close to the 1773 site of the Boston Tea Party. Costumed sailors act as guides, and you can even throw a bale of tea over the side (it is hauled back up again by an attached rope). An adjacent museum has an audiovisual presentation describing the events leading up to the Tea Party (*see p32 & p53*).
Congress Street Bridge. Tel: (617) 338 1773. Open: daily 9am–5pm. Admission charge. T station: South Station.

Bull and Finch Pub

Every day of the week people can be seen queuing for hours to enter this basement bar and restaurant. It is a curious phenomenon. The scriptwriters for the popular television programme called *Cheers* loosely based their series on the Bull and Finch. The exterior is shown briefly at the beginning of each episode, but the interior bears no relationship to the television stage set. Such is the power of TV that the pub attracts scores of pilgrims every day, many of them from overseas, but no one seems too disappointed at the difference. The bar food, in any case, is quite good, and there is plenty of atmosphere if you can manage to avoid the crowds.

84 Beacon St. Tel: (617) 227 9605. Open: daily 11am–2am. T station: Arlington.

Bunker Hill Monument, Charlestown

'Old Ironsides', the USS *Constitution*

Bunker Hill Monument

It was at Bunker Hill in 1775 that patriot Colonel William Prescott issued the famous command not to fire 'till you see the whites of their eyes'. Although the Redcoats ultimately seized the hill, over 1,000 British soldiers were killed in the battle, and the massive casualties were a severe blow. The battle is re-enacted annually on 17 June by costumed soldiers.

The monument, a 220-ft obelisk of granite from the nearby town of Quincy, has 295 steps leading to an observatory which has sweeping views of Charlestown and the navy yard, with Boston in the distance. At the foot of the monument is a small museum, The Lodge, with dioramas of the battle and weapons exhibited during the summer.

Monument Square, Charlestown. Tel: (617) 242 5641. Open: daily 9am–5pm (museum), 9am–4.30pm (monument). Closed: Thanksgiving, Christmas & New Year's Day. Free admission. Take the Orange Line to Haymarket T station, then bus 93 to Bunker Hill.

Charlestown Navy Yard

The navy yard's 30-acre site is part of the Boston National Historic Park. The yard was opened in 1800 to build and maintain ships for the US Navy, and it finally closed in 1974. The centrepiece of the site is the world's oldest commissioned warship still afloat. The USS *Constitution* – nicknamed 'Old Ironsides' – was built in 1794. It destroyed or captured 42 enemy ships, but was never defeated in battle. The public can go on board the ship.

Also in the yard is the USS *Constitution* Museum, which interprets the ship's history and the country's Federal period. The museum has several interactive exhibits and a resident model maker. The USS *Cassin Young*, a World War II destroyer, is also on exhibit in the yard.

Charlestown Navy Yard. Tel: (617) 242 5601. Open: daily 9am–5pm. Closed: Thanksgiving, Christmas & New Year's Day. Free admission (donations welcome).

Children's Museum

A giant milk bottle, now a Boston landmark, sits at the end of Congress Street Bridge on Museum Wharf. The bottle has been an outdoor refreshment stand since it was donated to the Children's Museum in 1977, and behind it is one of the most ambitious and extensive children's museums in the country. Four floors of exhibits cater for children of all ages, from toddlers to teenagers and beyond. Most of the exhibits are hands-on, and all offer learning and cultural experiences. There is an authentic Japanese silk merchant's house from Kyoto to explore, an exhibit

on multiculturalism that was the first of its kind, a 'Grandmother's Attic' where children can dress up in vintage clothes, and an extensive programme of special exhibits, events and performances (*see p53*).

300 Congress St. Tel: (617) 426 8855. Open: daily 10am–5pm, Fri till 9pm. Closed: Thanksgiving & Christmas. Admission charge. T station: South Station.

Vintage kitsch outside the Children's Museum: this 1930s fast-food stand is 40 feet tall

For years prior to the War of Independence, unrest and resistance to authority had been growing in Britain's North American colonies. Increasing taxes and trade restrictions, combined with no right to representation in Parliament, became a burden the Colonials were increasingly unwilling to bear. When a stamp tax was imposed in 1765, a group of Patriots formed the 'Sons of Liberty', dedicated to freeing America from Britain.

In 1770, in the then-occupied city of Boston, a belligerent mob was fired upon by British troops, and five

COL. SETH WARNER

Colonists were killed. The Boston Massacre, as it was soon called, was an indication of the violence to come.

Three years later, in 1773, a tax on tea pushed the Patriots over the edge. One dark December night, a group of 200 Boston merchants disguised themselves as Indians, boarded British ships, and quietly dumped 342 chests of tea into Boston Harbor. This 'Boston Tea Party' had grave consequences: the port was closed, the city was placed under martial law, and fresh British troops were quartered in private homes. A few months later, concerned at the growing atmosphere of rebelliousness, the general in charge of British forces in Boston decided on a show of force to overawe the Colonials. Seven hundred British regulars were ordered to march the 20 miles to Concord to seize illegal rebel military stores.

But the Patriots were unexpectedly well-organised. Two signal lanterns placed in the steeple of Boston's Old North Church told Paul Revere that the British were setting out for their Concord raid by boat from Boston Common. Revere then began his famous midnight ride to Concord to warn the Patriots to prepare for battle. When, on their way to Concord, the Redcoats arrived at Lexington early on the morning of 19 April 1775, they were met by a group of about 77 Minutemen – members of the citizen army who volunteered to be ready to fight at a minute's notice. The outcome was an easy victory for the British, who then marched the five miles to Concord. There they met hundreds more Minutemen. The North Bridge was the site of 'the shot heard round the world' – the first shot fired by an American in the War of Independence. The Redcoats began their return march around noon along Battle Road and were joined by 1,000 reinforcements at Lexington. Only this saved the British from complete disaster in their retreat back to Boston, through what now amounted to thousands of armed and determined Colonials.

Two months later, on 15 June, George Washington was appointed to command the army of the Continental Congress. The first great battle of the war took place just two days later on Breed's Hill north of Boston. After desperate fighting on both sides, the Americans fell back, defeated, to nearby Bunker Hill. In spite of this, the Americans considered the 'Battle of Bunker Hill' almost a victory, as their amateur, half-disciplined army of citizens had inflicted heavy losses on professional British troops, a high proportion of them officers.

Fighting continued south of New England in the mid-Atlantic and southern colonies, and in the midst of this, the Declaration of Independence was issued on 4 July 1776. The

Above: Paul Revere statue in Boston's North End; facing page: statue immortalising American Revolutionary Seth Warner and the Battle of Bennington

Revolutionary War was a long, drawn-out struggle which, in theory, the British should have won – and nearly did. But the decisive battle came in October 1781 at Yorktown, Virginia, when General Washington defeated General Cornwallis with the aid of the French, America's allies throughout the conflict. This victory ended the war, although British troops stayed on American soil for two more years before the Treaty of Paris, signed in September 1783, recognised American independence.

Chinatown

Chinatown lies immediately to the southeast of Boston Common adjoining the theatre district. Although rather small compared with other American Chinatowns, it is nevertheless authentically Chinese. The telephone booths are topped with pagoda roofs, street signs are in Chinese, and the neighbourhood is entered through a massive gate that was a Bicentennial gift from Taiwan. There is no shortage of restaurants, shops selling all manner of Chinese foods and spices, and even crates of live chickens for sale. The Chinese Cultural Institute, at 276 Tremont Street, has regular exhibits of Chinese arts and crafts, together with concerts and dramatic productions. Chinatown is actually expanding into what was once a seamy, violent area, now largely cleaned up.

Christian Science Center

Boston is the world headquarters of the Christian Science religion, founded by Mary Baker Eddy in 1879. A harmonious group of buildings has developed close to the Prudential Center. The original Mother Church (1894) was gradually joined by other buildings, culminating in the pedestrian plaza and reflecting pool. By far the most interesting exhibit at the Center is a 30-ft stained-glass walk-through globe, called the **Mapparium**, representing the world as it looked in 1935. Tour groups tend to visit in the mornings, so it may be better to avoid this time. A small window at the side gives a good view without having to wait. The globe is housed in the Publishing Society

On the Esplanade

Building, home of the *Christian Science Monitor*.
175 Huntington Ave. Tel: (617) 450 2000. Open: May–Oct Tue–Sat, 9am–4pm, Sun 11.15am–4pm; Nov–Apr Tue–Sat, 10am–4pm, Sun 11.15am–2pm. Free admission. T station: Symphony and Prudential.

The Esplanade

Bordering the Charles River from downtown to Back Bay is a wide green ribbon of much-used public park, with walking and cycling paths, benches and occasional children's playgrounds. It provides river access to boaters – a sailing school offers lessons and boat rentals to the public – a place to picnic or bask in the sun, and a venue for the Hatch Memorial Shell where the Boston Pops orchestra plays in free summer concerts. The shell – and the Pops – was made famous by its long-time and much-loved conductor, Arthur Fiedler, who is pictured in a monument there.

Copp's Hill Burying Ground

Boston's second oldest cemetery, dating back to 1659, played a significant role in the battle for independence. The British placed several guns here to fire on the Americans during the Battle of Bunker Hill, but to little effect. More devastating was the attack on Charlestown with incendiary shells. The British used the gravestones for target practice, and you can still see the marks left by musket balls on the gravestones of Grace Berry and Daniel Malcolm.

Hull and Snowhill Sts. Open: daily 9am–5pm. No convenient T station.

Faneuil Hall

The gold-plated grasshopper weather vane, modelled after a similar weather vane on London's Royal Exchange, has been spinning on top of Faneuil Hall since 1742. The hall was originally built as a market, but became known as the 'Cradle of Liberty' because of the patriotic speeches by Samuel Adams and James Otis at town meetings held on the upper floors.

The assembly room on the first floor is still used for town meetings, and it is worth a visit to view Daniel Healy's huge painting, *Liberty and Union, Now and Forever*, which dominates the room. On the top floor is the military museum and headquarters of the Ancient and Honorable Artillery Company of Massachusetts, America's oldest military organisation, chartered in 1638. National Park rangers give interpretative talks in the hall throughout the day.

Immediately behind Faneuil Hall is **Quincy Market**, a lively collection of eating places and shops, and one of the most popular attractions in the country.

Congress St. Tel: (617) 338 2323. Faneuil Hall and Quincy Market. Open: Mon–Sat 10am–9pm, Sun noon–7pm. Free admission. T station: Government Center/Haymarket.

The impressive façade of Faneuil Hall

Gibson House

Although this is one of the city's least-known museums, it gives the most complete picture of Victorian Boston. The house was built in Back Bay for Catherine Hammond Gibson in 1859, and it passed through three generations of this prominent Boston family before being opened as a museum in 1957. The house is a perfectly preserved Victorian time capsule full of absolutely authentic furniture, possessions and decorations. Not only can you experience the cluttered opulence of upper-class Boston, but also tour downstairs, the kitchen, pantries and laundry. Tours start on the dot; even if you are only a couple of minutes late, you will not be allowed inside.

Trinity Church, Copley Square

137 Beacon St. Tel: (617) 267 6338. Open: May–Oct Wed–Sun; Nov–Apr Sat–Sun. Tours start precisely at 1, 2 & 3pm. Closed: major holidays. Admission charge. T station: Arlington.

Globe Corner Bookstore

During the mid-19th century the Old Corner Bookstore (now restored and renamed) was the literary hub of Boston (*see p46*). Writers including Longfellow, Hawthorne and Emerson would regularly meet here, and both Charles Dickens and William Makepeace Thackeray stopped by on their visits to America. During this period, Tickner and Fields published works by Harriet Beecher Stowe, Thoreau, Browning, Julia Ward Howe, Emerson and many other prominent local authors, helping to establish a body of North American literature. Once threatened by urban renewal, it was saved by preservationists.
28 Church St, Harvard Square, Cambridge. Tel: (617) 730 3900. Open: Tue–Thur 10am–3.30pm. T station: State.

Institute of Contemporary Art

Housed in an old fire station, this Romanesque-style building hosts revolving exhibits on the cutting edge of modern art. The mixed media, video, performance and music events are often controversial and always stimulating. There is no permanent collection.
955 Boylston St. Tel: (617) 266 5152 for opening hours. T station: Hynes Convention Center.

Isabella Stewart Gardner Museum

This unusual and delightful museum, housed in a replica of a 15th-century Venetian palace, contains the personal collection of Isabella Stewart Gardner, amassed on her travels to Europe. The eclectic collection was personally arranged by Mrs Gardner, resulting in some bizarre and idiosyncratic displays. When she died in 1924, she willed that if anything was rearranged, then the entire contents of the museum should be sold and the monies given to Harvard University (fortunately, nothing has been touched!). The galleries, containing a priceless collection of fine and applied arts, all open on to a central courtyard full of greenery and fountains. All the great masters are represented here, with paintings by Rembrandt, Titian, Vermeer, Rubens, Raphael, Botticelli, Manet and Matisse, and the only fresco by Piero della Francesca outside Italy. From September to June, classical concerts are held in the Tapestry Room three times a week.

280 The Fenway. Tel: (617) 566 1401/ 734 1359 for concert information. Open: Tue–Sun 11am–5pm. Closed: Mon & national holidays. Admission charge. T station: Museum of Fine Arts.

John Hancock Observatory/ Prudential Tower Skywalk

The best view of Boston is from the 60th floor of the tallest building in New England. IM Pei designed the 740-ft high John Hancock Observatory in the late 1960s, and the 13 acres of mirror-glass walls have become a well-known city landmark. Adjacent to the Hancock is a topographical model of Boston as it

Isabella Stewart Gardner's home

was in 1775, complete with a Sound and Light show depicting the events of that fateful year. The show provides an excellent, dramatic introduction to the history of the city.

Photographers should be aware that the windows of the observatory have a tinted coating that is often scratched or distorted. Far better photographs can be taken from the observation deck of the Prudential Center, a short walk away (52 storeys).

John Hancock Observatory, 200 Clarendon St, Copley Square. Tel: (617) 247 1977. Open: daily 9am–6pm. Closed: Thanksgiving & Christmas Day. Admission charge. T station: Copley. Prudential Tower Skywalk, 800 Boylston St. Tel: (617) 859 0648. Open: daily 10am–10pm. Admission charge. T station: Copley or Prudential.

John F Kennedy Library and Museum

This dramatic building by architect IM Pei is situated on Columbia Point, with sweeping views of the ocean. Although several miles south of downtown Boston, it is nevertheless easily accessible. The Library is the official repository of all of Kennedy's presidential papers, and many of his personal belongings. It contains all of his speeches on film and video, and also the senatorial papers of Robert F Kennedy. (It is not generally known that the building also houses 95 per cent of the works of Ernest Hemingway.) This is not a library in the traditional sense. The visit starts with a 30-minute film on the life of Kennedy, followed by nine exhibits, many with video displays relating to JFK, including a recreation of the Oval Office in the White House. Leaving the exhibition, you will enter a glass meditation pavilion; beyond is an eight-storey tower where the archives are stored. These are available to the public for research.

Columbia Point.
Tel: (617) 514 1600.
www.jfklibrary.org.
Open: daily 9am–5pm.
Closed: Thanksgiving,
Christmas & New Year's
Day. Admission charge.
T station: JFK/U Mass
(then take the free transfer
bus, via the University of
Massachusetts, which leaves
every 30 minutes from
9am to 5pm).

John F Kennedy National Historic Site

This grandiose title refers to a small, insignificant house in the suburb of Brookline, restored to its 1917 appearance (when JFK was born there), and most of the contents belonged to the Kennedy family. The house where

John Fitzgerald Kennedy, political idealist; a hero still in a cynical age

THE KENNEDYS

In 1848 Patrick Kennedy arrived penniless in Boston from Ireland. He made money in saloons and banking, and became involved in local politics. His son Joseph married Rose Fitzgerald, the daughter of a long-time mayor of Boston.

Joseph had high political ambitions for his children, and when his eldest son, Joseph Jr, was killed in World War II, his younger brother John filled his shoes. After fulfilling his father's ambitions, serving three years as the 35th president of the United States, John was tragically assassinated in 1963. Five years later, his brother Robert suffered the same fate. The dynasty still hangs on, however, with Edward serving as a United States senator, and Robert's son Joseph's election to Congress in 1986. The remaining family still gathers regularly at the 'Kennedy Compound' at Hyannis Port on Cape Cod.

A visit to the JFK Library includes a film on the life of Kennedy

the Kennedys lived until 1920 is now run by the National Park Service, and has exhibits relating to Kennedy, and also a small bookshop. Of interest only to the most dedicated JFK fans, it is relatively inaccessible, and the JFK Library is of much more interest.
83 Beals St, Brookline. Tel: (617) 566 7937. Open: Wed–Sun 10am–4.30pm. Closed: Thanksgiving, Christmas & New Year's Day. Admission charge. T station: Coolridge Corner.

King's Chapel

George Washington, Revolutionary general and first president of the United States, used to attend services at this church. He also attended the musical entertainment that was planned to raise money for the new church building.

The original Anglican church was a wooden building. The present granite building was built around the original church, and the wood was removed piece by piece through the windows. Construction started in 1750, but the money ran out before a spire could be added. The oldest pulpit still in use on its original site overlooks an elegant Georgian interior.

Situated next to the church is Boston's oldest cemetery. Isaac Johnson, who owned the land, was the first person to be buried here in 1630. He was soon followed by several of the original colonists, including John Winthrop, the first governor of the colony. The writer Nathaniel Hawthorne used to frequent the cemetery, and it is thought that Elizabeth Pain, who was accused of adultery and buried here in 1705, provided the inspiration for the character of Hester Prynne in his book *The Scarlet Letter*.
58 Tremont St. Tel: (617) 227 2155. Church. Open: Mon & Sat 10am–4pm (summer), Sat 9am–4pm (winter). Donations welcome. T station: Park St.

Massachusetts General Hospital

A hospital may be the last place you would wish to visit on holiday, but this one has a glorious history. The modern hospital is considered to be one of the best in the United States, and its buildings cover several city blocks. However, it is the original building that is of particular interest.

The Bulfinch Pavilion, designed by Charles Bulfinch in 1816, is hidden in the centre of the modern maze. The best approach is from Cambridge Street to North Grove Street. The Greek Revival building sits incongruously surrounded by the new hospital and, surprisingly, is still in service as an active part of the hospital. The pavilion is topped by an elegant dome that houses what is now called the Ether Room, the hospital's operating theatre from 1821 to 1867.

It was in this room in 1846 that an operation was first performed using an anaesthetic – ether. Within a year, it was being used throughout the world. In 1869, Dr Joseph Lister introduced antiseptics to surgery in this same amphitheatre, and in 1886 the world's first appendectomy was performed, the first procedure involving the opening of the abdominal cavity. The Ether Dome is still in use today, but as a lecture hall. To visit the dome, enter the pavilion and pass through the hospital corridors to the rear lift (elevator), then follow the signs to the dome. If a lecture is in progress, the dome can be entered by a narrow stairway at the rear which leads to the top of the amphitheatre.
55 Fruit St. Tel: (617) 726 2000.
Open: during normal hospital hours.
Free admission. T station: Charles/MGH.

For discounted admission to a number of attractions, consider buying a CityPass. This is a booklet containing tickets to the following sights:

Museum of Science
New England Aquarium
Skywalk Observatory
Museum of Fine Arts
Harvard Museum of Natural History
John F Kennedy Library and Museum

A CityPass can be purchased for around $40 at any of the participating attractions, or in advance at *http://citypass.com*. It is valid for 1 year.

Museum of Fine Arts

Boston's premier art gallery is the equal of any gallery in the world, and it is certainly one of America's finest museums. The collections, spread out over two floors, are so exceptional that even a whole day spent here could only give a taste of its treasures. Certain exhibits, however, are important enough to top everyone's list. For a start, there is one of the greatest collections of Japanese art in existence. The basis of the collection was gathered by Edward Morse, Sturgis Bigelow and Ernest Fenollosa during their travels in Japan during the 19th century. The collection of Asiatic art as a whole is the largest of any single museum in the world. The collection from Egypt's Old Kingdom, the result of 40 years of excavation in conjunction with Harvard University, is second only to that in the Cairo Museum. Of particular interest in the fine arts exhibits is a superb collection of Impressionist paintings, including more than 40 by Monet. There are over

150 by Millet, among them his most famous work, *The Sower*, as well as Picasso's *Rape of the Sabine Women*. Twentieth-century painting is perhaps the weakest area, but even so there are impressive canvases by Jackson Pollock, Morris Louis, Robert Motherwell and Georgia O'Keeffe. In addition to the wonderful permanent collections, there are regular major touring exhibitions. *465 Huntington Ave. Tel: (617) 267 9300. www.mfa.org. Open: Mon & Tue 10am–4.45pm, Wed–Fri 10am–9.45pm, Sat & Sun 10am–4.45pm. Free repeat admission within 10 days. Closed: major holidays. Admission charge. Free guided tours. T station: Museum of Fine Arts.*

Museum of Science
This museum is a delight. It extends over two floors of a building located over the Charles River. There are over

The Museum of Fine Arts

140 exhibits, some dating back to 1830 when the museum was founded. Besides the traditional stuffed birds and dioramas, many interactive exhibits encourage the participation of inquisitive young minds. The perennial favourites are the world's largest Van de Graaff generator producing 15-ft bolts of lightning, the talking transparent women, and a 20-ft model of T Rex. There is also a 90-ft-long wave machine and a mathematics exhibit, interesting to even the most innumerate visitor.

Attached to the museum is the **Charles Hayden Planetarium**, which uses state-of-the-art, multi-image and projection equipment to portray astronomical phenomena or the night skies over Boston. The Mugar Omni Theater shows spectacular films on the 76-ft domed screen.
Science Park. Tel: (617) 723 2500. www.mos.org. Open: daily 9am–5pm; Fri till 9pm. Closed: Thanksgiving & Christmas Day. Admission charge. T station: Science Park.

Old State House

Old North Church, the oldest church in Boston

New England Aquarium

Appropriately located on Boston's waterfront (*see p52*), the aquarium has more than 70 exhibits showing aquatic life from around the world. The centrepiece is a huge, three-storey, 187,000-gallon tank, one of the largest in the world, around which spirals a walkway that gives intimate views of over 95 species of fish.

In 1999 the West Wing was completed, providing a 16,500-sq ft expansion for a changing exhibit area. The expansion also includes a 200-seat food service area, and a larger outdoor exhibit featuring seals and sea otters.

Next door to the aquarium, a floating theatre called Discovery presents dolphin and sea-lion shows throughout the day. *Central Wharf. Tel: (617) 973 5200. www.neaq.org. Open: Mon–Fri 9am–5pm, Sat, Sun & holidays to 6pm. IMAX 9.30am–10.30pm. Closed: Thanksgiving & Christmas. Admission charge. T station: Aquarium.*

Old Granary Burying Ground

Cemeteries may not seem the most pleasant places to visit, but the Old Granary Burying Ground is a virtual museum of Boston's – and indeed America's – history. Three of the signatories to the Declaration of Independence are buried here, including John Hancock. Here, too, are the graves of the five killed in the Boston Massacre, as well as Paul Revere, the parents of Benjamin Franklin and even Mother Goose! A map at the entrance indicates where the graves are thought to be. Unfortunately, the headstones were rearranged in the 1900s to 'improve' the cemetery's appearance, so it is impossible to know who is actually buried where. The headstones are particularly interesting because of their elaborate 17th-century carvings of skeletons, hourglasses and other suitably macabre motifs. *Tremont St, adjacent to Park St Church. Open: 9am–5pm. T station: Park St.*

Old North Church

Christopher Wren is thought to have inspired the design of this brick church, which is topped by a 175-ft, three-tiered steeple. It is the oldest church in Boston, built in 1723, and is certainly the most famous. On 18 April 1775, Robert Newman placed two lanterns in the belfry to signal to Paul Revere that the British army was advancing towards Concord. Revere's ride to Lexington and Concord to warn the Minutemen that 'the British are coming!' was immortalised in a poem by Longfellow.

The church itself has a beautiful, light interior filled with colonial history.

Brass plates on the pews indicate their former occupants; look for No. 54, which was the pew of the Revere family. On the left side of the vestibule as you leave the church, there is a tablet identifying 12 bricks from Boston, England, that have been set into the wall. They were taken from the prison cell that housed William Brewster and other Pilgrims who were imprisoned when they tried to flee the country in 1607. The bricks were given to the Old North Church by the Mayor of Boston, England, in 1923.

A small museum and gift shop are housed in a former chapel adjacent to the church. On display here is the 'Vinegar Bible', which was a gift from King George II in 1733. It got its name from a printing error which called the *Parable of the Vineyard* the *Parable of the Vinegar*.
193 Salem St. Tel: (617) 523 6676.

Open: daily 9am–5pm. Closed: Thanksgiving & Christmas Day.
T station: Haymarket.

Old South Meeting House
This church, which dates from 1729, is the second oldest in the city, and within its walls the Boston Tea Party was planned. Over 5,000 people gathered here in December of 1773 to protest against the despised tea tax imposed by the British (*see p46 & p50*). Audio tours of the church are available, and there are exhibits relating to many of the Meeting House's early congregation members, including black poet Phillis Wheatley, patriot Samuel Adams and Elizabeth Vergoose – the original Mother Goose.
310 Washington St. Tel: (617) 482 6439.
Open: Nov–Mar 10am–4pm, Apr–Oct 9.30am–5pm. Admission charge.
T station: State.

Old Granary Burying Ground

Old State House

Boston's oldest public building (*see p46*) dates back to 1713, and is now incongruously surrounded by modern commercial buildings.

Until the time of the Revolution, this was the colonial headquarters of the British Government. The British symbols of the lion and unicorn on the gables of the building are, however, copies, as the originals were burnt on 4 July 1776, when the colonies declared their independence.

Inside is an interesting little museum elaborating Boston's maritime history. Surprisingly, for such a historic monument, the T station has been located inside the building.

Directly across State Street is the National Park Visitor Center (*tel: (617) 242 5642*), which is not only a valuable source of information, but is also the starting point for ranger-led tours of the city. The centre also has good public toilets – a rarity in Boston. *206 Washington St. Tel: (617) 770 1713. Open: daily 9am–5pm. Closed: major holidays. Admission charge. T station: Government Center.*

Paul Revere House

This simple clapboard house is the last remaining 17th-century structure in Boston. Silversmith, engraver, printer and patriot, Paul Revere lived here from 1770 to 1800, and a few of the family's original furnishings remain. The Revere House is a major stop on the tourist circuit, and long queues often form to visit this tiny dwelling. *19 North Square. Tel: (617) 523 2338. Open: daily 9.30am–5.15pm (summer), 9.30am–4.15pm (winter). Closed: Mon Jan–Mar. Admission charge. T station: Haymarket.*

Paul Revere Mall

Set in the heart of Boston's North End, this tree-lined park has become a regular meeting place for the local Italian community. On summer afternoons, old men come out to gossip and enjoy a game of cards or checkers (draughts). The Mall, or Prado as the locals call it, is dominated at one end by a famous statue of Paul Revere on horseback (from which the mall derives its name), and, at the other, by the Old North Church. *T station: Government Center.*

MARITIME HISTORY

From the time the Pilgrims landed on Cape Cod, New England has had an intimate relationship with the sea. Whaling was the major industry during the 19th century, reaching its peak between 1820 and 1860, with large fleets in New Bedford and Nantucket.

Maritime commerce was always an important industry, from the infamous 'Triangle Trade' (molasses for rum for slaves) to the 'China Trade' out of the ports of Salem, Boston and Providence.

Today, maritime activity is mainly the preserve of leisure craft, and many thousands of recreational sailors ply the waters once ruled by the Captain Ahabs of the past.

Public Garden

The Public Garden is a continuation of the Boston Common, but the difference is immediately obvious. The Public Garden was the first botanical garden in the country, and is perfectly landscaped and manicured, with a weeping willow-fringed central lagoon. Boston's famous 'swan boats' have been a familiar sight on the lagoon every summer since 1877 when they were first introduced; they operate from April to September 10am–5pm (small charge). The garden also has a diverse collection of statuary depicting, among others, George Washington on horseback, and Mrs Mallard and her eight ducklings, a larger-than-life family much loved by children. In asking for directions to the garden, be sure to specify the *Public* Garden.
T station: Arlington.

State House

The golden-domed classical building crowning Beacon Hill was described by Oliver Wendell Holmes as 'the hub of the solar system'. It was designed by the great Boston architect Charles Bulfinch, and the cornerstones were laid by Paul Revere and Sam Adams in 1795. The interior is magnificent. The Hall of Flags, directly under the dome, was built to house a collection of Civil War battle flags; murals depicting Revere's ride and the Boston Tea Party decorate the Senate Staircase Hall, and floors throughout the building are made of 24 kinds of marble. In the House Chamber hangs a famous wooden fish, the 'Sacred Cod' of Massachusetts, which has been symbolising the importance of the fishing industry since 1784. In the basement archives and museum are copies of the Mayflower Compact, the State Charter granted by Charles I, and many other treasured historic documents. Entrance into the State House is via a side door. Only US presidents, or state governors leaving the House for the last time, have the privilege of using the main doors.
Beacon St. Tel: (617) 727 3676.
Open: Mon–Fri 9am–5pm. Tours: Mon–Fri every 30 minutes, 10am–3.30pm. Closed: state holidays.
T station: Park St.

The State House looks down onto Boston Common

Walk: The Freedom Trail

This is the perfect introduction to Colonial and Revolutionary Boston. Collect a free leaflet and follow the red line for 3 miles through the historic downtown area. *Although the walk merits a whole day, it can be completed in 3 hours. (See blue numbers on the map on pp24–5 for route.)*

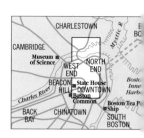

Start at the Park St T station. An information booth offers free maps and brochures about the trail.

1 State House

Cross the Boston Common to the State House (*see p45*).
Return along Park St, turning left at the church.

King's Chapel and Burying Ground

2 Old Granary Burying Ground

The cemetery is on the left (*see p42*).
Continue to School St.

3 King's Chapel and Burying Ground

These are located on the right corner (*see p39*). Continue down School Street. In front of the Old City Hall is a statue of Benjamin Franklin.
Continue to the end of the street.

4 Globe Corner Bookstore

The Globe Corner Bookstore (formerly the Old Corner Bookstore) is on the left corner (*see p36*).
Turn right into Washington St.

5 Old South Meeting House

The Meeting House is on the left (*see p43 & p50*). In front of the building is an excellent flower stand.
Return along Washington St and turn right into State St.

6 Old State House

This is opposite the National Park Visitor Center, which has an excellent bookstore and toilets (*see p44*).
Continue right on State St, past the Boston Massacre site. Turn left into Congress St.

7 Faneuil Hall and Quincy Market
Faneuil Hall is on the right (*see p35*).
Behind it is Quincy Market (a perfect
lunch stop).
From Faneuil Hall turn right into Union
St. Pass the Union Oyster House, on the
right; the new civic complex is nearby.
Turn right into Hanover St and cross
Blackstone St, with its weekly outdoor
market. Notice the brass fruit, vegetables
and rubbish set into the pavement. Pass
under the highway, turn right into Cross
St, turn first left, and continue to
Parmenter St. Turn right, then left into
North St.

8 Paul Revere House
This is on the left (*see p44*).
Continue up North St, turn left into
Prince St, then right into Hanover St.
St Stephen's is the only church designed
by Charles Bulfinch that remains in
Boston. Cross Hanover St and walk
to the end of Paul Revere Mall
(see p44).

9 Old North Church
The church is straight in front of you
(*see p42*). Leaving it, walk up Hull St
(excellent views from the top).

10 Copp's Hill Burying Ground
The cemetery gates are on the right
(*see pp34–5*).
You can finish here and visit Charlestown
separately, or continue down Hull St, then
left into Commercial St and right across
the Charlestown Bridge, to the Puritans'
first point of settlement, now called City
Square. Continue along Water St, where
Bunker Hill Pavilion has a good audio-
visual programme.

Faneuil Hall and Quincy Market

11 USS Constitution
The *Constitution* is in Charlestown Navy
Yard (*see p30*). Adjacent is the
Constitution Museum.
From this point, the red line is sometimes
obliterated, so ask for precise directions at
the museum.

12 Bunker Hill Monument
Sitting atop Breed's Hill, the monument
offers good views over the navy yard
(*see p30*). The trail ends here.
To return, walk down Lexington St for a
bus or taxi (no T service).

Walk: The African-American Heritage Trail

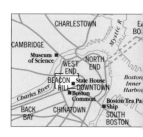

This trail celebrates the history of Boston's black community between 1800 and 1900, when they settled in this part of Beacon Hill (*see pp26–7*). It passes all the most interesting houses in the area and gives a glimpse of Victorian Boston. *(See green numbers on the map on pp24–5 for route.)*

The walk takes about 2 hours, including stops.

From Park St T station, cross the Boston Common towards the State House.

1 Shaw Memorial

Located opposite the State House in Beacon Street, this impressive bas-relief by Augustus Saint-Gauden honours the service of African-Americans in the Civil War. The first black regiment in the North was recruited in the state of Massachusetts and led by Shaw, a young, white, volunteer officer from Boston.

Walk down Beacon St, turn right into Joy St and left into Pinckney St.

2 Phillips School

This institution, at the corner of Anderson Street, was one of the first Boston public schools to have an interracial student body.

Continue on Pinckney St to No. 86.

3 John J Smith House

Smith was a distinguished black statesman who moved to Boston in 1848. A barber's shop owned by him was a centre of black abolitionist activity, and a meeting place for runaway slaves.

Continue down Pinckney St, turn left into West Cedar St, and right into Mount Vernon St. Walk down to Charles St.

4 Charles Street Meeting House

The Meeting House remained in use as a church until 1939, when it was the last black institution to leave Beacon Hill.

Continue down Charles St to Revere St, turn right, then left into West Cedar St, and right into Phillips St.

5 Lewis and Harriet Hayden House

This house, at No. 66, was a stop on the 'underground railroad' after the Fugitive Slave Law was passed in 1850. Lewis Hayden was eventually elected to the State Legislature, and Harriet Hayden established a scholarship fund for black students at Harvard Medical School.

Continue up Phillips St to the corner of Irving St.

6 Coburn's Gaming House

In 1844, John P Coburn founded this establishment as a private club that served as 'the resort of the upper ten who had acquired a taste for gambling'.

Turn left down to Cambridge St. Turn right and right again into Joy St, then right again into Smith Court.

7 African Meeting House

On the left at the end of Smith Court is the completely renovated African Meeting House, the oldest black church building (1806) in America.

8 Smith Court Residences

These are directly opposite the Meeting House, and they are typical of the homes occupied by black Bostonians throughout the 19th century.
Return to the corner of Joy St.

9 Abel Smith School

The first building in the nation built as a public school for black children, the 1834 school now houses exhibits and a museum shop.
Continue up Joy St to 5 Pinckney St.

10 George Middleton House

George Middleton was a colonel in the Revolution, and he commanded an all-black company. His is the oldest home to have been built by a black person on Beacon Hill.
This is the end of the trail. It is only a short walk back to Beacon St and the Boston Common.

The African Meeting House

Walk: The Women's Heritage Trail

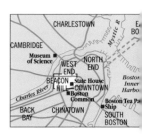

This trail, passing through Chinatown and the theatre district, highlights buildings where notable women have either lived or worked. *(See orange route on map on pp24–5.)* *The walk can easily be completed in 90 minutes.*

Start in Washington St.

1 Old South Meeting House
Displays feature the work of freed slave and poet Phillis Wheatley (an early member of the congregation), and that of historic preservationist Mary Hemenway *(see p43)*.
Leave the Meeting House, turn left and then left again into Milk St.

2 Milk Street
Writer Franklin Mecom lived at Nos. 15–17 Milk Street in the 18th century.
Return to Washington St and continue left through the downtown shopping area to West St. Turn right.

3 West Street
In the mid-19th century No. 13 was the bookshop of Elizabeth Peabody, who introduced kindergartens to New England.
Return to Washington St, turn right past the Opera Company of Boston founded by Sarah Caldwell, left into Ave de Lafayette, and right into Chauncy St, leading to Harrison Ave.

4 Harrison Avenue
At Nos. 2–8, Julia O'Conner led a successful strike of 8,000 women

telephone operators in 1919, paralysing the whole of New England for a week.
Continue down Harrison Ave to Beach St, turn left, then right into Tyler St.

5 Tyler Street
In 1761 the slave ship *Phillis* landed at Avery Wharf; among its human cargo was a child who became known as Phillis Wheatley, the first black female poet to be published in America. At No. 2 Tyler Street is the Chinese Women's Association, founded in 1942 in response to Madame Chiang Kai Shek's appeal for China relief. Number 76 was the home of the Lebanese-Syrian Ladies Aid Society, founded in 1917 to raise money for new arrivals and to provide relief to the Near East. Number 79 belongs to the Maryknoll Sisters of St Dominic, known for their service in China prior to the Communist takeover. They now serve worldwide, particularly in Latin America. Quincy School, at No. 90, opened in 1847 and, for the first time, American teachers had their own classrooms, and pupils their own desks. Although this was a boys' school, the teachers were women.
Continue to the end of Tyler St and turn right into Oak St.

6 Oak Street

The mural at No. 34 Oak Street symbolises Asian-American women in the garment industry.
Continue along Oak St to Tremont St and turn right.

7 Chinese Cultural Institute

The art gallery at No. 276 Tremont Street was founded in 1980 by Doris CJ Chu to promote racial harmony through cultural understanding. Plaques along Tremont Street theatre walls name famous actresses who have played there.
Turn left into Stuart St and walk through Transportation Building to Boylston Place.

8 Boylston Place

Number 5 is where the Boston Women's Trade Union League was based during the Great Depression.
Turn left into Boylston St to Park Square.

9 Park Square

From her office here, Pauline Hopkins edited *The Colored American* from 1900 to 1904.
Return along Boylston St to Tremont St, and turn left towards Boston Common.

10 Tremont Street

Number 174 was the Boston School of Cooking, the first professional school in Boston for women cooks. Fanny Farmer published her famous cookbook from here in 1896; it sold over 3 million copies.
Continue to Park St T station.

Flower seller outside the Old South Meeting House

Walk: The Boston Waterfront

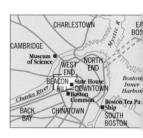

Since the founding of Boston, the waterfront has changed out of all recognition. Shipping is now reduced to ferries, sightseeing boats and pleasure craft; landfill has created a new, modern waterfront with good restaurants, where property is among the most expensive in the city. This walk illustrates some of the changes that have evolved over the centuries. *(See yellow route on map on pp24–5.)*
Allow 1½ hours.

Start at the Old State House (State St T station). Cross Congress St and walk down State St towards the water. Look for the Cunard sign at 126 State St; it is a reminder of the days when big ships came to Boston. Continue down to India St.

1 Custom House

This became the tallest building in Boston in 1915 when a 30-storey clock tower was added to the original Greek Revival building. In late 1996, it opened as a timeshare owned by Marriot Vacation Club. When open, the 25th-floor observation deck gives excellent views of the harbour and the financial district of the city.
Continue across Atlantic Ave.

2 Christopher Columbus Park

Opened in 1976, this park is ideal for a picnic, and for watching the harbour traffic, and the planes taking off from Logan Airport across the water. For picnic supplies, Quincy Market is only five minutes away.

3 Long Wharf

This is Boston's oldest wharf, dating back to 1710, and before landfill it extended for half a mile up State Street, almost to the Old State House. In its day it was the major centre of activity for seagoing voyages and delivery of cargo. Views from the end of the wharf are as sweeping as ever.

4 New England Aquarium

Just one wharf over from Long Wharf, the aquarium continues to be one of Boston's favourite attractions (*see p42*). Sit for a while and watch the harbour seals in their outdoor pool by the entrance.
Continue south along the waterfront.

5 Rowes Wharf

The 1987 Rowes Wharf complex, with its huge six-storey arch, houses a luxury hotel, apartments, offices and shops. The water-shuttle to Logan Airport leaves from here, and it is worth taking the seven-minute trip just to experience its picturesque approach to the city.

Continue alongside Atlantic Ave, turn left into Northern Ave, and cross the bridge. Turn right into Sleeper St.

6 Children's Museum
The Children's Museum can be identified by a 40-ft milk bottle, actually a fast-food stand (*see p31*).
Cross Congress St Bridge.

7 Boston Tea Party Ship
Halfway across the bridge on the right is the Boston Tea Party Ship. The original location has long since vanished to landfill, but the ship is a full-scale working replica with a small, lively museum (*see p29*).

Continue across the bridge and turn left into Dorchester Ave, then right into Summer St. Continue to Atlantic Ave.

8 South Station
When it was completed in 1900, this was the biggest railway station in the world. Most of the original granite construction has been demolished, but the impressive entrance remains. The present building is a sensitive and carefully executed effort at restoration. The cavernous terminal is bustling with cafés, vendors and shops.
The walk ends here, and there is a T station at South Station.

The Children's Museum has attractions for kids of all ages

New England is a living museum of the history of American architecture, from the earliest colonial styles to contemporary modernists. In Boston the name Charles Bulfinch occurs with predictable regularity. He was New England's most prolific architect during the early 1800s, designing both residential and civic buildings, culminating in the Capitol Building in Washington DC. The architecture of the region falls into six periods.

Early Colonial

The first houses built in New England were simple, wood-shingled cottages with classical symmetry, usually mixing medieval design elements such as an overhanging second storey and a massive central chimney. Often a 'lean-to' was added, resulting in the New England 'saltbox' that can still be seen all over Cape Cod.

Georgian

By the end of the 1700s, greater prosperity created a demand for larger, more spacious houses, and the elegant Georgian architecture of England was introduced first to Boston, as early as 1686, and much later elsewhere in New England. These symmetric brick or wooden buildings, with hipped roofs and careful, stripped detail, were built to the exact standards of proportion developed during the Italian Renaissance. Earlier casement windows lost favour and were replaced by sash windows with smaller rectangular panes.

Federal

This post-Revolutionary extension of the Georgian style was more delicate, with many design features inspired by England's Adam brothers. A unique feature of this New England architecture was the balustrade surrounding the roof on houses built near the sea. This 'widow's walk' gave seafarers' wives a high vantage point from which to look out for their husbands' boats.

Greek Revival

Rounded arches, shallow domes and low pitched pediments are all features of this style that was based on the temples of ancient Greece. It was popular in the southern part of New England for civic and commercial buildings; Boston's Quincy Market is a good example.

Victorian

The Victorians developed many different schools of architecture. One of the most nationally influential, known as Richardson Romanesque, used massive stonework and powerful arches. The style lives on in libraries and city halls throughout the nation. Gothic Revival also reared its head during this period, producing houses covered in the ornate trim that was now so easily made with machinery.

Stained glass was also widely used, as were polychrome bands of tile and brickwork. The Beaux Arts movement brought the new Renaissance to New England, and the strong French influence can be seen in many mansions in Newport, Rhode Island.

Contemporary

New England boasts a who's who of contemporary architecture. The great Bauhaus architect Walter Gropius left Germany in 1937 and moved to Harvard as Director of the School of Architecture. Since then virtually every major architect has designed at least one New England building. IM Pei's work seems to be everywhere, and there are several buildings in the Boston and Cambridge areas by Eero Saarinen, Philip Johnson, Louis Kahn and James Stirling.

Facing page: Classic New England church architecture; below: a rich architectural heritage exposed, Boston after the expressway

Cambridge

Although their histories have long been intertwined, Cambridge is a separate city from Boston. Green lawns, towering trees, red-brick quadrangles, the Charles River with people sculling along its sweeping curve – all are set off by an invigorating 21st-century atmosphere, young, bustling and trendy. Newtowne, as it was first called, was established in 1630, and became the first capital of the Massachusetts Bay Colony. In 1636 a college was founded – the first in America, later to become Harvard – for the purpose of training young men for the ministry (*see p64*). That same year the town was renamed Cambridge, after the town in England where many of the Puritans had completed their studies.

Memorial Hall, Harvard

In 1639 the first printing press in the New World was established in Cambridge, and the document *The Oath of the Free Man* became the very first American publication.

In 1916 the prestigious Massachusetts Institute of Technology (MIT) left Boston and crossed the river; together with Harvard University, it forms one of the premier seats of learning in the

Harvard Square, centre of intellectual ferment

Cambridge

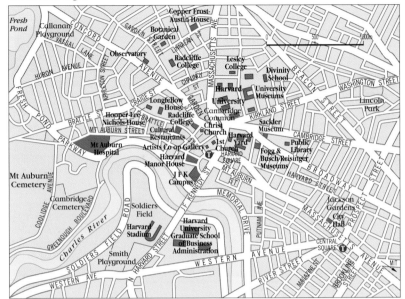

world. Today, Cambridge exudes an academic atmosphere – which is not surprising, since almost half of its 96,000 population is involved in education and the universities.

The heart of Cambridge is Harvard Square (actually a triangle). In the centre of the square is the landmark Out of Town News, with newspapers and magazines from every corner of the globe. Most of the major sites are within easy walking distance of the square.

Brattle Street

The wealthy Loyalist Tories of the 18th century built grand houses along the western end of Brattle Street, giving it the name Tory Row. Fine examples are the Ruggles Fayerweather House at No. 175 and the Hooper-Lee-Nichols House at No. 159.

Christ Church

Built in 1760, this simple grey and white building – the oldest church in Cambridge – sits on the edge of Cambridge Common. A brass plaque marks the pew where George Washington and his wife worshipped on New Year's Eve in 1775.

On the wall of the vestibule is a bullet hole which is believed to have been fired from a British rifle as the Redcoats marched on their way to Lexington. Under an elm tree on the Common, a plaque marks the exact spot where General Washington took command of the Continental Army in 1775. Close by are three British cannons that were abandoned at Fort Independence.

Garden St. Tel: (617) 876 0200.
Open: daily 9am–5pm. Free admission.

Harvard University

The whole of Cambridge revolves around this venerable institution. The university has over 400 buildings spread over 380 acres of land. There are seven museums and more than a hundred libraries.

Sculling on the Charles River

Harvard Yard

The Yard is the oldest part of the campus. Walk across from Harvard Square and enter the first quadrangle. On the western side of the Yard is Massachusetts Hall. It was built in 1720, and is the oldest Harvard building still standing.

Opposite is the famous statue of John Harvard by Daniel Chester French. The inscription 'John Harvard, Founder 1638' has earned the statue its nickname, 'The Statue of Three Lies': French used a student, not Harvard himself, as a model for the statue; John Harvard was not the founder, but a benefactor; and the college was founded two years earlier, in 1636.

The Yard is a series of interconnected squares, each surrounded by academic buildings dating from the early 1700s to the present day. These green oases offer a tranquil alternative to the bustle of Harvard Square.

Arthur M Sackler Museum

British architect James Stirling designed this Post-Modern building, which was completed in 1986. It houses a remarkable collection of ancient Asian and Islamic art, including some of the world's finest Chinese jade. There is also a particularly good collection of

Japanese woodblock prints. The Harvard University art museum shop is located here, and special exhibitions are also featured throughout the year.
485 Broadway. Tel: (617) 495 9400.
Open: Mon–Sat 10am–5pm, Sun 1–5pm.
Free tours daily at 1pm. Admission charge (includes Fogg and Busch-Reisinger Museums). Free admission on Wed & Sat from 10am–noon.

Busch-Reisinger Museum

This museum includes a unique collection of 20th-century German art, particularly the Expressionist movement. Other periods of German and some Eastern European art are also represented, along with decorative arts, architectural drawings and sculpture.
32 Quincy St. Tel: (617) 495 9400.
Open: Mon–Sat 10am–5pm, Sun from 1pm. Admission charge (includes Fogg and Sackler Museums). Free admission on Wed & Sat from 10am–noon.

Fogg Art Museum

This gallery, founded in 1891, is the oldest of the Harvard art museums. The galleries are on two levels surrounding an Italian Renaissance courtyard, and contain a comprehensive collection of Western art. Particularly notable are the Impressionist paintings and British Pre-

Raphaelite works. Concerts are often held in the central courtyard.

A gallery of decorative arts has displays of furniture, clocks, china and so on, from Harvard's vast collection. Included here is the president's Chair, brought to Harvard in the mid-1700s by the Reverend Edward Holyoke, and used during commencement ceremonies by every Harvard president since.

32 Quincy St. Tel: (617) 495 9400. Open: same as Busch-Reisinger Museum. Free tours daily at 11am & 2pm. Admission charge (includes Busch-Reisinger and Sackler Museums). Free admission on Wed & Sat, 10am–noon.

Museums of Natural History

Four distinct museums share the same building in Oxford Street (*see box on p61*

for practical details). As they are in the middle of the University complex, parking is next to impossible. However, there are parking meters exclusively for museum visitors just off Oxford Street, and there is usually space available.

Botanical Museum

If there is time to visit only one museum in this fascinating complex, then it has to be the Botanical Museum. The centrepiece here is the remarkable 'Garden in Glass'. Between 1887 and 1936, over 840 species of plants and flowers were made entirely from glass by brothers Leopold and Rudolf Blaska. Sadly, sonic booms shattered a few of the models; the 700 or so exquisite 'plants' are displayed in glass cases, in an appropriately Victorian atmosphere.

Harvard University's buildings stand proud throughout the city

John Harvard's statue

Geological and Mineralogical Museum

This comprehensive collection of rocks, minerals and crystals has a distinctly Victorian feel to it. The most interesting specimens are the giant gypsum crystals from Mexico, and a 3,040-carat topaz.

Museum of Comparative Zoology

This traditional collection of fossils, bones and stuffed animals has a number of highlights. The Thayer Hall displays every species of bird that breeds north of Mexico. There is the world's oldest egg, laid 225 million years ago. Skeletons of the 25,000-year-old Harvard mastodon and the coelacanth (the fish thought to have been extinct for 70 million years but recently rediscovered) are also on display.

Peabody Museum of Archaeology and Ethnology

Founded in 1866, this is the oldest cultural museum in North America. It boasts one of the most important collections of American Indian culture in the world – the result of many Harvard-sponsored expeditions to North, Central and South America – and some items were brought back by the Lewis and Clark Expedition of 1804–6. The Mayan collection is particularly strong. Throughout the museum, dioramas represent different tribal habitats.

Memorial Church

The church facing the Widener Library was built as a memorial to the men of Harvard who died in World War I. It contains one of the great Baroque organs of America, built by CB Fisk.

Widener Memorial Library

The Widener Memorial Library impressively overlooks the second quadrangle of the Yard. This modern, Corinthian-colonnaded building, dating back only to 1913, is home to the third-largest library in the whole of North America, with countless manuscripts and first editions. It also houses the only remaining volume from John Harvard's collection.

In 1764 a massive fire destroyed the 5,000-volume library which contained his complete collection. One single volume had been borrowed by a student the night before the fire. When he returned the book, according to legend, the president profusely thanked the student – and then expelled him for taking the book without permission!

The library was named after Harry Elkins Widener, a Harvard alumnus of 1907, whose parents donated funds to complete the building in 1915. Young Harry went down with the *Titanic* because, the story goes, he returned to his cabin to rescue a first edition of Francis Bacon's essays. In the Harry Elkins Widener Memorial Room there is a display of his collection, which includes one of the remaining 50 Gutenberg Bibles, and a first folio of Shakespeare dating back to 1623. There are also dioramas showing Cambridge in 1667, 1775 and 1936, and murals by John Singer Sargent in the stair hall. Non-students are not allowed to enter the book collections, but the steps and yard are well worth the visit.

Harvard Yard. Tel: (617) 495 4166.
T station: Harvard.

Museums of Natural History
24 Oxford St. Tel: (617) 495 2326 (Botany); tel: (617) 495 4758 (Minerals); tel: (617) 495 2463 (Zoology); tel: (617) 495 2248 (Peabody). Open: daily 9am–5pm. Admission charge.

The 19th-century Memorial Hall at Harvard contrasts with the late 20th-century Science Center

Maclaurin Building, Massachusetts Institute of Technology

MIT

Main Exhibition
Center, 265
Massachusetts Ave.
Tel: (617) 253 4444.
Open: Tue–Fri 10am–5pm,
Sat and Sun noon–5pm.
Admission charge.
Compton Gallery, Hart
Nautical Galleries,
77 Massachusetts Ave.
Tel: (617) 253 4444.
Open: **Hart** *daily*
9am–8pm; **Compton**
Gallery *Mon–Fri*
9.30am–5pm. Free
admission. T station:
Central.
List Visual Arts Center,
20 Ames St. Tel: (617)
253 4680. Open:
Tue–Thur, Sat and Sun
noon–6pm, Fri noon–
8pm. Free admission.
T station: Kendall.

Longfellow National Historic Site

This magnificent Georgian dwelling, with sunny yellow clapboarding, shutters and grand entrance, was used by George Washington as his headquarters during the siege of Boston in 1775–6. It is now operated by the National Park Service.

Henry Wadsworth Longfellow, who taught at Harvard, rented a room here in 1837, and when he married wealthy heiress Fanny Appleton, his father-in-law gave them the house as a wedding gift. Theirs was a happy marriage, and they had six children, but Fanny died tragically after 18 years when her hooped skirt caught fire – she was melting sealing wax to preserve locks of their children's hair. Longfellow, bearing dreadful facial scars from his attempts to save his wife, continued to live in the house for a further 27 years. He wrote many of his best-known poems here, including *Paul Revere's Ride*, *The Song of Hiawatha* and *Evangaline*, and visitors included Dickens, Twain, Emerson, Hawthorne and Wilde.

The furnishings are virtually as they

were in Longfellow's time, and visitors can see his study, many of his personal possessions, and hundreds of books from his library, as well as the Steinway piano, around which he enjoyed singing the German song, *Leider*.

105 Brattle St. Tel: (617) 876 4491. Open: Wed–Fri noon–4.30pm; Sat & Sun 10am–4.30pm, summer Wed–Sun 10am– 4.30pm. Closed: Christmas, Thanksgiving & New Year's Day. Admission charge.

Massachusetts Institute of Technology (MIT)

Quite the opposite of Harvard – in its architecture and atmosphere, as well as geographically – MIT has been representing the best education in engineering and technology since 1861. Set on the banks of the Charles River, the modern campus and its geometrical buildings, designed by the likes of Eero Saarinen and IM Pei, form a suitable reflection of the Institute's emphasis on high tech.

The MIT Museum is actually a group of four museums, all of which complement the more traditional approach of the Harvard museums.

The **Main Exhibition Center** houses a collection of architectural plans, photographs, scientific instruments and other artefacts relating to the Institute. There are interactive plasma globes, mathematical sculptures, holography exhibits, demonstrations of photo-micrography and many other fascinating examples of the frontiers of science.

The **Compton Gallery** has exhibits showing the interaction between art and science, while the **Hart Nautical**

Galleries contain a renowned collection of ship models, plans, marine art and engine models.

In **Strobe Alley** there is an exhibition of the work and equipment of scientist and photographer Harold Edgerton, an MIT faculty member who was a pioneer in the use of stroboscopic lighting.

The MIT **List Visual Arts Center** has three galleries displaying the most interesting art in a variety of media.

Radcliffe College

Radcliffe was founded in 1879 to permit Harvard professors to teach women who were not allowed admission to Harvard as students. Its name honours Lady Anne Radcliffe Mowlson, a 17th-century British benefactor of Harvard who established that college's first scholarship. Longfellow's daughter, Alice, was instrumental in the college's foundation.

Radcliffe remained a sister institution to Harvard until 1975, when the administrations were merged, and equal admission standards were adopted for both men and women.

Entering the Radcliffe campus off Brattle Street, visitors discover graceful old school buildings surrounding a delightful landscaped quadrangle with a perfect lawn.

Of all the buildings at Radcliffe, the most important is the **Schlesinger Library**, which houses the largest and most comprehensive collection of women's literature in the country. The library contains the archives of many notable women, including suffragists Susan B Anthony and Julia Ward Howe.

The Collegiate School of Saybrook, founded by Harvard graduates in 1701, moved to New Haven, Connecticut, in 1716. Two years later it was renamed Yale after its benefactor, Elihu Yale.

In 1755 the Reverend Eleazar Wheelock founded Moore's Indian Charity School in Hanover, New Hampshire. The name was changed to Dartmouth College in 1769. Tuition is still free to members of the Six Nations Confederation.

In 1764 Nicholas Brown, a prominent Rhode Island merchant whose family had made their fortune in the China trade, founded Rhode Island College as a Baptist school. In 1804 the name was changed to Brown University.

Thus, the foundation of Ivy League education was established.

The Puritans realised that higher education was an essential foundation on which to build their ideal society. As a consequence, New England has a greater concentration of first-class universities than any part of the country. The traditional academic atmosphere of these venerable institutions can be traced directly back to the Oxford or Cambridge roots of their founders.

Newtowne College was founded in 1636 primarily to train young men for the Puritan clergy. The name was changed to Harvard College two years later, after John Harvard died and bequeathed his library of 400 books and half his fortune to the college. Many US presidents, including both Adamses, both Roosevelts and John F Kennedy, were Harvard graduates.

In complete contrast are the many new concrete-and-glass technological universities that have mushroomed in the last century, building on the firm traditional scholastic base already in place. Heading the list – although dating from 1861 – is the Massachusetts Institute of Technology (MIT), with many other colleges close behind.

Altogether there are 269 colleges and universities, 7.5 per cent of the total for the whole United States. In the Greater Boston area alone there are 65 well-established academic institutions.

Facing page: Harvard University; above and right: Massachusetts Institute of Technology

Lexington and Concord

West of Boston, these two towns are carved indelibly into the American story as the 'Cradle of Liberty' – the place where the first shots of the American Revolution were fired. In addition to its historic interest, Concord is a major stop on the New England literary trail (*see p70*) as home to several major 19th-century writers.

Concord's First Parish Meeting House

Concord

To most Americans Concord and Lexington (*see pp68–9*) are inextricably linked to one another. Although close to one another geographically and historically, Concord has both greater charm and greater vitality than Lexington, and a much broader range of sights to visit.

On 19 April 1775, after the confrontation at Lexington, the British marched on to Concord, where 400 Minutemen waited near the Old North Bridge. They forced the British into a retreat to Boston in what was the first serious battle of the American Revolution.

The **Concord Museum** contains 15 period rooms and galleries that present local history through decorative arts and domestic artefacts. Displays include the contents of Emerson's study, the simple furniture from Thoreau's Walden Pond cabin and one of the lanterns that signalled to Paul Revere.
200 Lexington Rd. Tel: (508) 369 9609. Open: Jan–Mar, Mon–Sat 11am–4pm, Sun from 1pm; Apr–Dec, Mon–Sat 9am–5pm, Sun from noon. Admission charge.

The **Minuteman National Historical Park** visitor centre shows films and exhibits relating to the battle. Walk

The Wayside, home of Nathaniel Hawthorne

down to the Old North Bridge (a modern replica) and the Daniel Chester French statue of a Minuteman, made from a melted 1776 cannon.
Start at Battle Rd Visitor Center, off Route 2A on Airport Rd. Tel: (978) 369 6993. Open: daily 8.30am–sunset; extended summer hours.

Literary Concord
A short walk from the Old North Bridge is the **Old Manse**. Ralph Waldo Emerson lived here for a period, then the house was occupied by Nathaniel Hawthorne for two years while he was writing *Mosses from an Old Manse*. The house is full of Hawthorne and Emerson memorabilia and original furniture.
Monument St. Tel: (508) 369 3909.

Emerson moved to the **Ralph Waldo Emerson House**, where he lived from 1835 to 1882. The restored house is furnished as it was during his time.
28 Cambridge Turnpike.
Tel: (508) 369 2236.

Hawthorne, who wrote *The House of Seven Gables* and *The Scarlet Letter*, lived for some time at **The Wayside** after buying it from the Alcott family.
455 Lexington Rd. Tel: (508) 369 6975.

The Alcotts moved on to **Orchard House** and lived here for almost 20 years. Louisa May wrote both *Little Women* and *Little Men* here.
399 Lexington Rd. Tel: (508) 369 4118.

The other major figure in the Concord Group, as they called themselves, was Henry David Thoreau, whose *Walden* has become an American classic on environmentalism. For two years he lived a life of contemplation and reflection on nature in a cabin by

Old North Bridge, Concord

Walden Pond. The **Thoreau Lyceum**, headquarters of the Thoreau Society, has a replica of that cabin and an extensive library and collection of memorabilia.
156 Belknap St. Tel: (508) 369 5912.

Walden Pond Reservation lies on Route 126 just across Route 2 from Concord. It was here that Thoreau wrote *Walden*. Today a cairn marks the site of his cabin, and there is boating, fishing, swimming and a picnic ground.

You can reach Concord Depot by Commuter Rail trains, but it's a long walk to the literary sites. The Boston History Collaborative, *www.literarytrailofgreaterboston.org*, runs tours from Boston.

Opening times and days vary with the season. Phone for details. The writers' houses, which all charge admission, are open daily from mid-April to Oct, from about 10am–5pm; Sun usually from 1pm. The **Lyceum** also charges an admission fee; it is open year round 10am–5pm; Sun from 2pm. **Walden Pond**, open all year 5am–sunset, is free but charges for parking.

Lexington

The village green, still surrounded by 18th-century buildings, has not changed much in appearance since 1775. The British, planning to overawe the restive Colonials with a show of force, were marching from Boston to Concord. Paul Revere's midnight ride had alerted the Patriots, and the Minutemen mustered on the village green before dawn.

The exact location of that fateful first skirmish on 19 April is marked with a statue of Captain John Parker, commander of the Minutemen. A boulder is inscribed with his command: 'Stand your ground. Don't fire unless fired upon, but if they mean to have a war, let it begin here.' A shot was fired, no one knows by whom, and by the battle's end eight of the 77 Minutemen were killed. The best place to start a visit is at the Lexington Visitor Center.
1875 Massachusetts Ave. Tel: (781) 862 1450. Open: May–Oct, daily 9am–5pm; rest of the year, 9am–3.30pm. Free admission.

Buckman Tavern

Next to the Visitor Center is Buckman Tavern, where the Minutemen waited through the night after Paul Revere's warning. The tavern, built in 1709, looks exactly as it did in April 1775.
Hancock St. Tel: (781) 862 5598. Open: mid-Apr–Oct, Mon–Sat 10am– 5pm, Sun from 1pm. Admission charge.

Hancock-Clark House

John Hancock's father built this house in 1700. It was here that Sam Adams and John Hancock hid after being warned of the British advance by Paul Revere.

Both men were wanted by the British for their opposition to the Crown.
36 Hancock St. Tel: (781) 861 0928. Open: mid-Apr–Oct, Mon–Sat 10am– 5pm, Sun from 1pm. Admission charge.

Munroe Tavern

The Munroe Tavern served as field headquarters and hospital for the British in their retreat from Concord. It has been restored to its original appearance.
1332 Massachusetts Ave. Tel: (781) 674 9238. Open: mid-Apr–Oct, Mon–Sat

Massachusetts

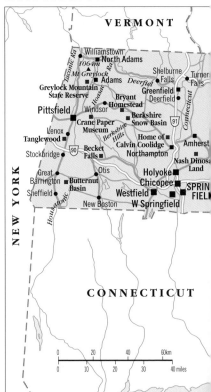

10am–4pm, Sun from 1pm.
Admission charge.

Museum of Our National Heritage
This modern brick and glass building
has numerous displays illustrating the
country's history from colonial times.
Permanent exhibits include swords,
clocks and furniture from different eras.
Weekly programmes include a variety of
films and concerts.
Route 2A and Massachusetts Ave.
Tel: (781) 861 6559. www.monh.org.

*Open: Mon–Sat 10am–5pm, Sun from
noon. Free admission.*

Minuteman statue, Concord

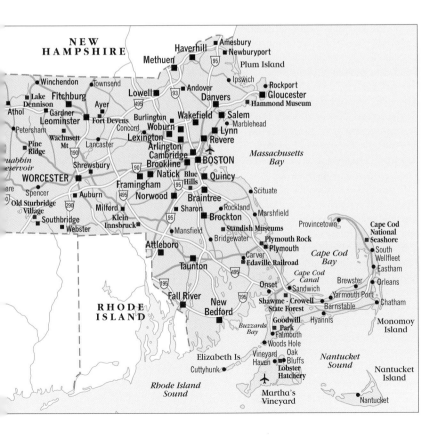

Literary New England

New England's literary traditions began in the 1600s with the poetry of Anne Bradstreet, and have continued to flower ever since. It was Noah Webster of Hartford, Connecticut, who in 1828 wrote the first dictionary of American English, still the most widely used. Webster was responsible for removing the superfluous 'U' from colour, honour and harbour.

Home of horror genre novelist Stephen King

Perhaps the most prolific literary period was in the mid-1800s, when essayist Ralph Waldo Emerson led a philosophical movement known as Transcendentalism, embracing the idea that all nature was united. The circle of literary luminaries that lived near him in Concord, Massachusetts included Henry David Thoreau, Nathaniel Hawthorne (*The Scarlet Letter, House of the Seven Gables*) and Louisa May Alcott (*Little Women*). You can visit the homes of Emerson, Alcott and Hawthorne, as well as Walden Pond, immortalised by Thoreau.

In nearby Cambridge, the poet Henry Wadsworth Longfellow was a professor at Harvard and you can visit his home there and his family home in Portland, Maine.

Both Edgar Allen Poe and Benjamin Franklin were born in Boston, but moved out of New England before their literary careers got underway. Poe returned briefly to Providence, Rhode Island, where he often read in the Athenaeum. Here, too, he courted the librarian, for whom he wrote 'To Helen'. Inspired by Poe was the later master of dark tales, HP Lovecraft, of Providence.

Although the best-known writings of Samuel Clements (whose pen name was Mark Twain), including *The Adventures of Tom Sawyer,* recall his boyhood home along the Mississippi, from the age of 35 he lived and worked in Hartford, Connecticut. His neighbour there was Harriett Beecher Stowe, author of the classic 'propaganda novel' *Uncle Tom's Cabin.* President Abraham Lincoln, when introduced to her, said, 'So this is the little woman who started the big war.' The Stowe and Clements homes are open to the public, as is the summer home of Herman Melville, in Pittsfield, Massachusetts, where he wrote *Moby Dick.*

Later literary figures include the poets Amy Lowell of Boston, Emily Dickinson of Amherst, Massachusetts and Edna St Vincent Millay of Camden, Maine. Dickinson's home is now a museum. Pulitzer Prize-winning dramatist Eugene O'Neill was from New London, Connecticut.

The quintessential New England – perhaps American – poet is Robert Frost, whose works often refer to life in the region. Two of his New Hampshire homes are open, in Derry (near the southern border) and Franconia, in the White Mountains.

The best-known New England novelist today is certainly Stephen King. In his home town of Bangor, Maine, you can tour sights referred to in his books, and see his home with its unique bat-and-spiderweb fence.

THE NORTH SHORE

The North Shore of Massachusetts is an unspoiled stretch of rugged coast and seaports that has escaped excessive commercialisation.

Gloucester

Gloucester, 40 miles northeast of Boston, is the oldest fishing port in the nation. The town's fishing industry is still important, and gained wide attention as the subject of the bestseller, *The Perfect Storm.* On Western Avenue is the famous Fishermen's Memorial, *Man at the Wheel*, in memory of '[They] that go down to the sea in ships'. Harbour tours and whale-watch cruises are available from the wharfs.
Cape Ann Chamber of Commerce (main information centre on the North Shore), Commercial St. Tel: (978) 283 1601.

Marblehead

The protected harbour at Marblehead, 18 miles northeast of Boston, attracted fishermen from Cornwall who settled here in 1629. The harbour is one of New England's most popular among today's pleasure sailors. Several very fine 17th- and 18th-century houses line the winding streets of the old part of town. Historic sights include **Abbot Hall**, the old town hall in Washington Square (*tel: (781) 631 0528*), and the **Jeremiah**

Lee Mansion at 161 Washington Street (*tel: (617) 631 1069*).
Chamber of Commerce, 62 Pleasant St. Tel: (781) 631 2868.

Rockport

A few minutes north of Gloucester, on Route 127, is one of the most painted and photographed harbours in America (a lobster shack here has earned the nickname 'Motif No 1'). This extremely picturesque area has become almost an icon for the New England fishing port.

Rockport itself is a charming fishing village on the rocky promontory of Cape Ann. Long a favourite with tourists, it has nevertheless been developed with restraint and good taste, and its quaint atmosphere retained.
Chamber of Commerce, 3 Main St. Tel: (978) 546 6575.

Shacks and jetties extend into Rockport harbour, famed for its scenery, shops, restaurants and galleries

Salem

A few miles north of Marblehead, on Route 1A, Salem was once one of America's most infamous towns. Founded in 1626 by Roger Conant, Salem became the most Puritan of Puritan towns. Roger Williams was driven from here for his liberal beliefs and went on to found Rhode Island. The zealots of Salem continued to purge the town of perceived evil-doers, leading to the witchcraft hysteria of 1692 (*see box*).

But there is far more to the town than gruesome executions. Salem went on to become a major trading port and seafaring centre. During the late 1700s ships began trading with China and the Far East, and this led to the birth of the China trade.

House of the Seven Gables Historic Site

Nathaniel Hawthorne immortalised this 1668 house in his novel of the same name. It has been restored to its appearance in Hawthorne's time, and a film describes how the house inspired him to write his novel. Also on the grounds are three other historic houses, period gardens and panoramic views of Salem Harbor. *54 Turner St. Tel: (978) 744 0991. www.7gables.org. Open: daily 10am–5pm, off season varies. Admission charge.*

Peabody Essex Museum

The Peabody Essex Museum is the oldest museum in continuous operation in the United States, founded in 1799 to exhibit 'natural and artificial curiosities' that had been collected on voyages of Salem ships around the world.

There are four major collections in the museum, all of them related to maritime matters and international commerce. Over 300,000 items are housed in seven buildings, with over 30 galleries. The Asian Export Art Collection is a unique collection of objects that were made in Asia for export between 1500 and 1940. There is a maritime history collection, a natural history exhibit, and the Japanese collection is one of the most important in the world. Visit the three beautifully restored houses operated by the museum in chronological order, to get a feel for the changes in

THE SALEM WITCH HUNTS

For a brief period in the 1690s, Salem was in the grip of a hysteria that began simply enough with tales of the supernatural. A young girl, with two of her friends, was listening to these tales told by Tituba, the West Indian slave of a minister. When, later, the girl began babbling and convulsing, she was diagnosed as being bewitched, and all three girls accused Tituba and two other women of witchcraft. Over the following months, 19 people were hanged, and one was crushed to death with rocks. The witch hunt stopped when suspicion fell on the Governor's wife, and he released all the accused from jail.

lifestyle over 150 years – the **John Ward House** built in 1685, the **Crowninshield-Bentley House** dating back to 1727 and the **Garneer-Pingree House** of 1805.
132 Essex St. Tel: (978) 744 3390.
East India Square. Tel: (978) 744 3390.
www.pem.org. Open: daily 10am–5pm.
Admission charge.

Stephen Philips Trust House

For a sense of a real Salem family's evolution from the China trade days to the 20th century, visit this historical home filled with the collections of five generations of the Philips family. The exhibition rooms explore post-war inventions and daily life.
34 Chestnut St. Tel: (978) 744 0440.
Open: Jun–Oct, Mon–Sat 10am–4.30pm.
Admission charge.

Salem Maritime National Historic Site

This includes the 2,000-ft long Derby Wharf, the Bonded Warehouse and the Custom House (immortalised in *The Scarlet Letter*). The West India Goods Store sells items similar to those on sale in 19th-century Salem, such as coffee, tea, spices and porcelain.
174 Derby St Waterfront. Tel: (978) 740 1660. Open: daily 9am–5pm.
Closed: Thanksgiving, Christmas Day & New Year's Day. Admission charge.

Salem Witch Museum

Set in an 1840s church, the museum graphically recounts the chronology of the witch hunt in an elaborate Sound and Light show with 13 life-size tableaux that take you hauntingly back to those times. Children especially love this macabre exhibit.
191/2 Washington Square North. Tel: (978) 744 1692. Open: daily 10am–5pm, Jul–Aug 10am–7pm. Admission charge.

The Witch House

This 1642 dwelling was the home of Judge Jonathan Corwin, who presided at the witch trials. The interior has been restored to its original appearance in 1692, when over 200 women accused of witchcraft were brought here to the judge's chamber.
310 Essex St. Tel: (978) 744 0180.
Open: daily May–early Nov 10am–5pm, call for extended Oct hours.
Admission charge.

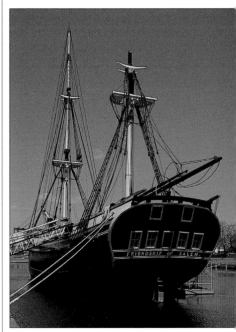

Sloop *Friendship* at Salem Maritime National Historic Site

South Shore and Cape Cod

Access to the Cape has always been difficult, and this prevented the development of mass tourism until the road to Provincetown was completed in 1938. Cape Cod was never the same again. It has achieved an almost mythical reputation as an idyllic seaside destination, which attracts almost 4 million tourists every summer. Before June and after August the area returns to a more leisurely pace, and the wild beaches can be experienced in something like their natural state. The islands of Nantucket and Martha's Vineyard are reached by ferry from Hyannis or Woods Hole, or by air for short domestic connections. Each island is small enough for a day trip.

For information visit www.capecodchamber.org

Brewster
There are two interesting attractions for children along Route 6A (which in Brewster becomes Main Street). The **Cape Cod Museum of Natural History** has a working beehive, nature trails and a weather station. The **New England Fire and History Museum** has displays of old fire-fighting equipment dating from the late 1700s, accompanied by the sounds of old firebells and alarms, plus a Victorian apothecary shop, herb garden and blacksmith shop.
Cape Cod Museum, Route 6A. Tel: (508) 896 3867.

www.ccmnh.org. Open: daily 10am–4.30pm, seasonal hours vary. Admission charge.
Fire and History Museum, Route 6A. Tel: (508) 896 5711. Open: Mon–Fri, 10am–4pm, Sat–Sun from noon. Closed: Columbus Day–Memorial Day. Admission charge.

Eastham
Cape Cod National Seashore stretches from Orleans all the way to the far northern tip of the Cape. Some 27,000 acres of dunes, glacial cliffs, woods, marshes and ponds have an extensive network of

DRIVING THE CAPE

Cape Cod is, technically speaking, an island by virtue of the Cape Cod Canal, which effectively separates the arm of the Cape from the mainland. Route 6 crosses the canal on the Sagamore Bridge and continues on to Provincetown at the far tip of the Cape.

Route 28 crosses the Bourne Bridge and continues to points along the south shore. It leads to the ferry to Martha's Vineyard.

The best way to reach Cape Cod is on Route 6A – a more attractive and atmospheric approach to the Cape than the southern route.

Route 28 through Hyannis consists of cheap motels, fast-food outlets and gas (petrol) stations.

Route 6A splits off from Route 6 shortly after crossing the Sagamore Bridge. A string of charming small towns such as Sandwich, Yarmouth and Brewster lines its north shore.

nature trails and bicycle trails giving access to this wild coastal landscape. The Salt Pond Visitor Center, on Nauset Bay near Eastham, has plenty of literature on the seashore, together with maps and trail guides. Guided walks and lectures are offered.

Exit 18 off Route 6A. Tel: (508) 255 3421. Open: all year (seashore); daily early Mar–2 Jan (visitor centre). Free admission but parking charge.

Martha's Vineyard

Martha's Vineyard, which was President Bill Clinton's favourite holiday spot, is one of the most fashionable summer retreats in America (*see pp80–81*). Jackie Onassis had a house here, as do many entertainment celebrities, and although the island is only 20 miles long by 10 miles wide, the famous faces manage to avoid the 65,000 visitors that come over every summer.

The island is undeniably attractive. Picture-perfect small towns like Edgartown sit in scenery reminiscent of the Irish coast. Commercialism has by and large been avoided, and the only major concessions to tourism are the mopeds that buzz around the island, much to the annoyance of residents.

Nantucket

The island of Nantucket, 30 miles off the Massachusetts mainland, is more remote and even smaller and less developed than Martha's Vineyard. The town of Nantucket (*see pp82–3*) has an old-world charm that has been preserved to perfection. Outside the main town there is a village at either end of the island; Madaket to the west and Siasconset, which is particularly attractive, to the east. There are good beaches all round the island.

Dunes at Head of the Meadow beach, Cape Cod National Seashore

Plymouth

Plymouth lies just off the main road from Boston to Cape Cod, and on no account should the short detour be missed. The town is full of early American history (*see pp84–5*), and visitors can gain a remarkable insight into the lives of the Pilgrims.

Cranberry World

Plymouth and Cape Cod are the habitat for one of America's native fruits, the cranberry, which grows in low-lying bogs. Every September and early October, when the bogs are flooded, lakes of brilliant red cranberries colour the countryside. Ocean Spray's Cranberry World has exhibits of equipment, historic photographs and a small working cranberry bog – plus opportunities to sample their products. If the cranberry theme catches your imagination, drive along Route 58 about 10 miles to Carver, cranberry capital of the world. In the autumn there are cranberries as far as the eye can see.
225 Water St. Tel: (508) 747 2350. Open: daily 9.30am–5pm May–Nov. Admission charge.

Mayflower II

In 1620 the original *Mayflower* made the voyage from England in 66 days. The three-masted merchant vessel had previously been in the fish trade with Norway and, after that, in the wine trade with France. The 102 passengers, Puritan refugees from religious intolerance, left England and 102 arrived in the New World – one dying at sea and one being born (appropriately named Oceanus Hopkins).

The full-scale reproduction of the original *Mayflower* made the eventful 44-day voyage from England in 1957 under full sail. The *Mayflower II* now sits in Plymouth Harbor, where you can talk with guides about the history of Plymouth Colony, life on board the original *Mayflower*, wooden ship-building and the ongoing restoration of *Mayflower II*. Entering the ship, you can browse through exhibits about New England's native people and the voyage of the *Mayflower II* from England.
State Pier. Tel: (508) 746 1622 or (800) 262 9356. Open: daily 9am–5pm. Closed: Dec–Mar. Admission charge.

Plimoth Plantation

Three miles south of the *Mayflower II* lies Plimoth Plantation, a site that is almost totally cut off from the modern age (the only intrusion being the visitors and occasional aircraft flying overhead).

From the Visitor Center, the walk to the actual settlement takes several minutes, but the effect is remarkable. Once the car park and modern buildings of the Visitor Center are well out of sight and sound, the path rounds a corner into an unpaved street. Suddenly it is 1627. A complete village, authentic in every detail, descends down the slope towards the sea. Chickens run about, Pilgrims tend gardens and work on the buildings, and the women often wear corsets to give them the correct period shape. At lunch time, families sit around the table eating 17th-century meals cooked over wooden fires. The actor-interpreters speak in 17th-century English, and if it were not for all the

21st-century visitors the illusion would be complete. This is interpretive living history at its best.

Adjacent to the Plantation is **Hobbamock's Homesite**, a Wampanoag Indian home consisting of two simple shelters and two or three Indian interpreters who depict a very different culture from the Pilgrims', but in an equally lively and informative way. The settlement is within the Plimoth Plantation complex and does not require a separate entrance fee. The best times to visit Plimoth Plantation are early in the week, either first thing in the morning or late in the afternoon. *Route 3A, Warren Ave. Tel: (508) 746 1622 or (800) 262 9356. www.plimoth.org. Open: daily 9am–5pm, Apr–Nov. Admission charge.*

Time stands still at Plimoth Plantation

Provincetown

At the very northern tip of the Cape sits Provincetown, where the Pilgrims made their first landfall in 1620. The 252-ft **Pilgrim Monument** commemorates the event, and is a spot for excellent views of the Cape. It is also home to a museum which includes native artefacts and historical pieces.
High Pole Hill Road. Tel: (508) 487 1310. Open: daily Apr–Nov 9am–4.15pm, with extended summer hours.

After the Pilgrims came the whalers and fishermen, and Provincetown remains an active fishing port. Today the whales attract viewers instead of hunters, fortunately, with a wide choice of cruises leaving from MacMillan Pier.

In the early 1900s Provincetown was discovered by artists and writers, including playwright Eugene O'Neill. This love affair has faded. Today, Provincetown is a mixture of interesting history and the elements of tourism. The tiny city is perhaps best known for its diverse population and exciting nightlife, rich with artists, unique shops, comedians and fantastic drag shows. There is never a dull moment in 'P-Town'! There is a visitor centre right off MacMillan Pier.
*Chamber of Commerce, 307 Commercial St. Tel: (508) 487 3424.
www.ptownchamber.com*

Sandwich

Sandwich, situated at the western end of Route 6A, has more sights on the Cape than any other town. Slow growth has helped keep its original character intact. A lovely place, it is built around Shawme

Beachgoers at Herring Cove, Cape Cod

Pond, an artificial lake that provided water power for milling.

Dexter's Gristmill

Next to the pond is a mill that was in use from the 1650s until the late 19th century; it is still used for practical demonstrations of old corn-milling techniques.
Main St. Open: mid-Jun–early Oct, Mon–Sat 10am–5pm, Sun from 1pm. Admission charge (with Hoxie House).

Heritage Plantation

These 76 acres of gardens to the east of Sandwich form one of the most ambitious historical complexes in New England. Formerly the estate of horticulturist Charles Dexter, who specialised in the propagation of rhododendrons, the gardens are a blaze of colour from mid-May to mid-June. Reproductions of historic buildings house several different collections. The

Vintage Car Museum, in a replica of the famous round barn in Hancock Shaker Village (*see pp88–9*), has cars dating from 1890 to the beginning of World War II, including Gary Cooper's 1931 Duesenberg. Other buildings have displays of firearms, miniature military paintings, folk art and a 1912 carousel.
At Grove and Pine Sts. Tel: (508) 888 3300. Open: mid-May–mid-Oct, daily 10am–5pm. Admission charge.

Hoxie House

Close to the mill is what claims to be the oldest house on the Cape (1637). This restored grey saltbox is complete with authentic 17th-century furnishings.
Water St. Tel: (508) 888 1173. Open: as for Dexter's Gristmill. Admission charge (with Dexter's Gristmill).

Sandwich Glass Museum

Deming Jarves founded the Boston and Sandwich Glass Company in the centre of the village in 1825. The materials he needed to operate efficiently and economically were here, and he believed his workers would be less distracted if they were away from the fleshpots of Boston. The formula worked. Sandwich glass, using a Roman three-part moulding method, became famous and is now highly valued by collectors for its subtle colours. The museum has an extensive collection of original pieces and a diorama illustrating glass-making.
Town Hall Square. Tel: (508) 888 0251. Open: daily Apr–Oct 9.30am–5pm; rest of the year, Wed–Sun 9.30am–4pm. Closed: Jan. Admission charge.

Thornton W Burgess Museum

Almost next door to Hoxie House is the small cottage that was home to the naturalist and author whose children's books included *Peter Cotton Tail* and *Old Mother West Wind*. The museum contains his writings, personal mementoes and original illustrations.
4 Water St. Tel: (508) 888 4668. Open: Mon–Sat 10am–4pm, Sun from 1pm. Closed: Easter, Thanksgiving & Christmas Day. Donations welcome.

Heritage Plantation, Sandwich

Tour: Martha's Vineyard

Martha's Vineyard is the ideal place to see by bicycle. There is an excellent network of bike paths, it is relatively flat apart from the Up-Island area, and small enough to cover in a day. The ferries carry cars as well as foot passengers, but during the summer it is far better, and cheaper, to leave cars on the mainland. Ferries arrive at either Vineyard Haven or Oak Bluffs, and several bike rental shops are visible as soon as you disembark. Rented mopeds (for which a driving licence is required) are not popular.

Allow 3 hours.

1 Vineyard Haven

This is the port most visitors use. A short walk from the docks, on Beach Road, is the Martha's Vineyard Chamber of Commerce (*tel: (508) 693 0085* or *(800) 505 4815*), where you can find excellent maps and other information on the area. Although never overly popular with tourists, the town has had a loyal following of writers since Lillian Hellman and Dashiell Hammett stayed here in the 1930s.

Take Beach Rd out of town and follow the coast past East Chop Lighthouse to Oak Bluffs.

2 Oak Bluffs

Oak Bluffs was the first place on the island to become popular with tourists. The town is famous for the Oak Bluffs Campground, off Circuit Avenue, where there is a 33-acre cluster of Gothic Victorian holiday cottages.

Take Sea View Ave out of town past the town beach. A paved bike path follows the coast.

3 Joseph Sylvia State Beach

This sandy beach beside calm waters has good views towards Cape Cod. For sea bathers and casual strollers there are always vendors with a varied assortment of fast food.

Continue on the bike path.

4 Edgartown

Edgartown is the most elegant town on the island, with expensive boutiques, fine restaurants and 17th- and 18th-century sea captains' houses. On Cooke Street, stop by the **Thomas Cooke House** (nothing to do with this book!), where the Martha's Vineyard Historical Society (*tel: (508) 627 4441*) has historical background on the island and a walking-tour guide. The house itself is one of the Society's exhibits, illustrating the island's history through the eyes of a customs collector who lived here in the late 18th century.

For an interesting side trip take the bike path along Katama Rd for about three miles to Katama Beach.

5 Katama Beach

Sometimes called South Beach, this has the best windsurfing on the island. Swimming can be dangerous on this three-mile stretch, but during the summer there are plenty of beach activities including informal sandcastle competitions.

Return to Edgartown and take the Edgartown–West Tisbury Rd.

6 Manuel F Correllus State Forest

This cool, hushed forest in the centre of the island has almost 4,000 acres of pine, scrub oak, ponds and streams. A bike path, on which mopeds are prohibited, circles the forest. There is a two-mile nature trail through the forest for those with enough energy.

Continue around the forest on the bike path and take Airport Rd to join the

Edgartown Light

Vineyard Haven–Edgartown Rd. Return to Vineyard Haven.

During the summer, the narrow roads become very crowded. Be careful of both other traffic and loose gravel and sand. Every year there are cycling accidents on the island.

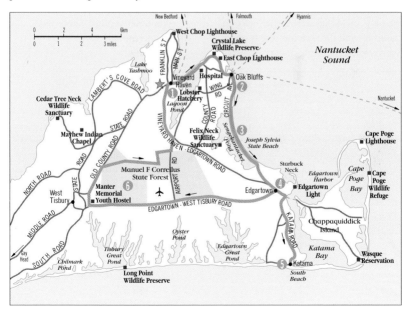

Walk: Nantucket

In the 19th century Nantucket was the world capital of the whaling industry. But with the discovery of petroleum in 1859, demand for whale-oil plummeted, sending Nantucket into a slow decline that succeeded in preserving its character. It remains one of the most picturesque towns imaginable. The island's name came from the Indian word *nanticut*, meaning 'faraway land', and it still takes over two hours on the ferry from Hyannis. Even if only for a day, it is well worth a visit to this New England outpost.

Leaving the Steamboat Wharf ferry terminal, walk down Broad St.

1 Whaling Museum
On the right-hand side of Broad Street, this old whale-oil candle factory now has displays relating to the history of whaling, including scrimshaw, harpoons, paintings and the skeleton of a 46-foot sperm whale. Recently re-opened after a 12-million dollar restoration.
Turn left into South Water St and continue to Main St.

2 Main Street Square
This charming, cobblestoned square is the heart of town, where it is easy to feel part of another century. Shops and galleries intermingle with old sea captains' homes.

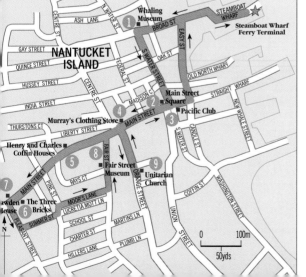

3 Pacific Club
At the foot of the square, this old seamen's club (private) is still active as a place where mariners can tell tall tales or play a game of cribbage. The Chamber of Commerce at 48 Main Street has a good supply of literature and maps of the island.
Walk up to Main St.

4 Murray's Clothing Store
It was here that Rowland

Macy left the family business, joined a whaling ship, went prospecting for gold in California, and finally founded RH Macy & Co, one of America's biggest department store chains.
Continue to 75 & 78 Main St.

The ferry landing, Nantucket

5 Henry and Charles Coffin Houses

These two wealthy brothers built identical houses facing each other. Charles was a simple Quaker, but notice the more flamboyant embellishments of Henry's house, particularly the cupola on the roof and the white marble trim round the front door.
Continue to 93, 95 & 97 Main St.

6 The Three Bricks

These three identical houses were built in the 1830s by Joseph Starbuck for his three sons. This astute businessman retained the title to the houses to ensure that the sons stayed in the family business.
Cross to 96 Main St.

7 Hawden House

This Greek Revival mansion is the only house on the tour open to the public. The elegant interior illustrates how wealthy 19th-century merchants lived (William Hawden was himself a merchant and also a candle-maker who owned the factory that now houses the

Whaling Museum). The house is open only during the summer.
Turn left into Pleasant St, left into Summer St, and continue on to Moor's Lane; turn left into Fair St.

8 Fair Street Museum

On the left, next to the Quaker Meeting House, this museum displays paintings of Nantucket by contemporary as well as 19th-century artists. It is the art museum of the Nantucket Historical Association.
Continue down Fair St, turn right into Main St, and right again into Orange St.

9 Unitarian Church

This 1809 building is one of the most beautiful on the island, and its golden dome has long been a landmark for seafarers. Notice the *trompe l'œil* panelling inside.
Return to the starting point, along Main St to Easy St, then turn right back to Steamboat Wharf.

Walk: Plymouth

Few places in New England have so much authentic history concentrated into such a small area. This walk includes several historic houses dating back to the 16th and 17th centuries, and all are open to the public. A route is suggested for the walk, but the sites are so close together that a leisurely day could be spent just wandering at random from museum to museum.

Allow 1½ hours, longer for museum visits.

Start on Water St on the seafront.

1 Plymouth Rock

What more suitable place could there be to begin than the point where the Pilgrims first set foot ashore in 1620? Plymouth Rock is enshrined in a Neo-Classical building that is considerably more impressive than the rock itself!
Continue north on Water St to State Pier.

2 *Mayflower II*

This is an accurate re-creation of the ship that brought the Pilgrims from England to New England. It is staffed by guides who talk about the history of Plymouth Colony, life on board the original *Mayflower*, and the ongoing restoration of the *Mayflower II*.
Cross Water St and walk up North St, past the Pilgrim Mother Fountain on the right, to Winslow St.

3 Mayflower Society House

The tour of this house, built in 1754, covers two distinct periods. The front is authentic 1754 Colonial, while the rear is 1898 Victorian. Ralph Waldo Emerson was married here in 1835, and ether was discovered in this same house in 1842.
Cross North St.

4 Spooner House

Generations of the same family lived in this house for over 200 years, from 1749 to 1954. It is now a museum furnished with Spooner family heirlooms.

Map not to scale

*Return along North St towards the sea
and turn right into Carver St.*

5 Plymouth National Wax Museum

The only wax museum in New England,
with scenes telling the Pilgrims' story.
*Continue down Carver St passing Coles
Hill, the burial ground for the first
settlers. Cross Leyden St to Brewster
Gardens and view the Pilgrim Maiden
Statue. Follow the brook to Water St, and
proceed to Sandwich St.*

6 Howland House

Members of the Pilgrim group once
lived here. There are good displays of
17th- and 18th-century furnishings,
and the house is charmingly staffed by
costumed hostesses.
*Cross Pleasant St to Summer St and
continue to Spring Lane.*

7 Richard Sparrow House

This 1640 house hosts demonstrations
by local craftsmen in the craft shop.

*Walk down Market St, then School St,
past the Burial Hill overlooking the
harbour. Turn right into South Russell St
and left into Main St, which turns into
Court St. Walk five blocks to Chilton St.*

8 Pilgrim Hall Museum

The nation's oldest public museum, built
in 1824, houses the most complete
collection of Pilgrim artefacts and
possessions.

There is the cradle of the first baby
born in the new colony, paintings by the
Pilgrims, books, manuscripts and
household utensils.
*Continue up Court St and turn right on
Memorial Drive.*

9 Hedge House Museum

An interesting costume and fashion
display can be seen in this fine example
of a merchant's home from the early
1800s. There is also some fine English
china from the same period.
Return to Plymouth Rock along Water St.

This grand structure protects Plymouth Rock, the Pilgrims' stepping stone into the New World

Western Massachusetts

Two major valleys extending from Vermont to Connecticut divide the western half of Massachusetts. The Pioneer Valley follows the course of the Connecticut River, and the Berkshire Valley follows the Housatonic River.

Historic Deerfield

Amherst

Amherst, 25 miles north of Springfield, is an attractive, small academic community that is home to the University of Massachusetts, Hampshire College and Amherst College, as well as to both Noah Webster, of dictionary fame, and the poet Emily Dickinson. Amherst was founded in 1821, and its Victorian architecture lines the southern side of Amherst Common. With a student population of just 1,600, it is one of the smallest Ivy League colleges. *Chamber of Commerce, 409 Main St. Tel: (413) 253 0700.*

Emily Dickinson House

Dickinson was born in this house and died here too. After her father's death in 1874, she left the house only once, when her nephew died next door. She wrote nearly 1,800 poems while she lived here, although only ten were published during her lifetime. The rest, in neatly bound sheafs, were found by her sister after Emily's death in 1886. *280 Main St. Tel: (413) 542 8161. Guided tours on the hour 1–4pm Wed–Sat, and Sun Jun–Aug. Admission charge.*

Mead Art Museum

The Mead has an excellent collection of 19th- and 20th-century American art, as well as artefacts, paintings and sculpture from the 17th to the 20th century. *Amherst Campus, Route 116. Tel: (413) 542 2335. Open: Mon–Fri 10am–4.30pm, weekends 1–5pm; out of term, Tue–Sun 1–4pm. Free admission.*

Pratt Museum of Natural History

The museum has the world's largest mastodon skeleton, together with a large collection of local geological specimens. *Amherst Campus, Route 116. Tel: (413) 542 2165. Open: Mon–Fri 9am–3.30pm, Sat 10am–4pm, Sun noon–5pm; out-of-term hours are limited, phone for information. Free admission.*

Deerfield

Deerfield was settled in 1669 as a frontier outpost. In the Bloody Brook Massacre of 1675 the town lost 64 men in a fight with the Indians during King Philip's War. In 1704 the French led about 350 Indians on a dawn raid, killing 49 people in five hours, burning half the town, and leading 112 prisoners on a winter death march to Canada. Settlers returned in 1706, and Deerfield developed into a small but prosperous agricultural centre.

Historic Deerfield

This is considered one of the best-preserved Colonial districts in New

England, and ranks with the greatest historic preservation areas in America. The first restoration project of its kind in the country is a single mile-long street (The Street), lined by 65 18th- and 19th-century houses, of which 12 are open to the public. Both the interiors and exteriors are completely authentic. Houses are open only for scheduled tours, which makes it almost impossible to see more than just a few in one day.

The **Ashley House** was the home of the Reverend John Ashley, who moved here in 1732, and contains a fine collection of 18th-century furniture from New England.

One of the earliest dwellings is the 1720 **Frary House**, later converted to a tavern, complete with ballroom and fiddlers' gallery.

The **Helen Geier Flynt Textile Museum** houses a collection of textiles, coverlets, needlework and clothing in an 1872 barn.

The **Henry N Flynt Silver and Metalware Collection** includes pieces by Paul Revere, as well as English and American pewter and silver, and a re-creation of an 18th-century silversmith's shop.

The **Sheldon-Hawks House** (1740) is one of the best-preserved 18th-century buildings. It has a good furniture collection and an engaging, beautifully restored kitchen.

The **Stebbins House** dates back to 1799 and was extended in 1810. Exotic French wallpaper illustrates Captain Cook's South Sea voyages.

The **Wells-Thorn House** illustrates how life changed through increasing prosperity, its seven rooms arranged chronologically from 1725 to 1850.
Information Center, Hall Tavern. Tel: (413) 774 5581. Open: daily 9.30am– 4.30pm. Closed: Thanksgiving & Christmas Day. Tours: 10am–4pm. Admission charge.

Memorial Hall Museum
The museum contains a collection of Colonial, American Indian and military relics, as well as a replica of a 1797 schoolroom and a display of pewterware. A door still has a hatchet hole in it, a grim reminder of the fateful day of the French-led Indian raid.
Memorial St. Tel: (413) 774 3768. Open: May–Oct, daily 9.30am–4.30pm. Admission charge.

Risen from the ashes of 1675, Deerfield's present buildings are lovingly preserved

THE SHAKERS

Lenox

South of Pittsfield, in the Berkshire Hills, is an area that became known as the 'Inland Newport' because of the extravagant 'cottages' built there by wealthy families. Some of these estates in Lenox and nearby Stockbridge (*see p92*) are open to the public.

The Mount

The Mount was the summer home of author Edith Wharton. The exquisite Gothic Revival mansion was built in 1902 and is currently under-going major restoration, although it remains open to the public. Dramatic productions are presented here during summer. *Plunket St. Tel: (413) 637 1899. Open: daily May–Oct 9am–5pm. Tours available at no charge.*

Tanglewood

For many people Lenox is synonymous with Tanglewood, the summer home of the Boston Symphony Orchestra. Out-door concerts are given on the beautiful, 210-acre estate during the months of July and August, and attended by musicians from all over the world. *Hawthorne Rd. Tel: (617)*

266 1492 before mid-Jun, or (413) 637 5165 after mid-Jun. www.bso.org

Pittsfield
Arrowhead

Just south of Pittsfield is Arrowhead, the home of Herman Melville, author of *Moby Dick*. From the study window there is a fine view of Mount Greylock, which reminded Melville of the great whale, Moby Dick. *780 Holmes Rd. Tel: (413) 442 1793. Open: daily Jun–Nov 9.30am–5pm, last tour at 4pm. Admission charge.*

Hancock Shaker Village

This is one of the finest Shaker settlements in

The movement started in the north of England in 1747 as a branch of the Quaker religion. During church services, religious fervour caused their bodies to tremble and shake. They became known as the 'Shaking Quakers' and thus the 'Shakers'. In 1774; Ann Lee of Manchester, England, founder of the Shakers, ventured to the New World to escape religious persecution. She established the first Shaker community at Watervliet, New York.

Hancock's round Shaker barn, built in 1826, has the austere beauty of a masterpiece

A demonstration of hand-made preserves at Hancock Shaker Village

existence. The round barn, built in 1826, is a masterpiece of functional design; one man standing at the centre of the barn could feed 54 cows at once. The village ceased being an active community in 1960, and since then 20 buildings have been restored. Interpreters demonstrate 19th-century skills such as woodworking, blacksmithing and Shaker cooking.
US 20 (5 miles west of Pittsfield), junction of Routes 20 & 41.
Tel: (413) 443 0188. Open: end May, Memorial Day weekend–Oct, daily 9.30am–5pm; Apr–May & Nov 10am–3pm. Admission charge.

Springfield

Springfield is a large industrial town that had one of the country's first motor car factories (1895). Nowadays the city's main claim to fame is the invention of basketball. The first game was played at Springfield College in 1891.

Naismith Memorial Basketball Hall of Fame

The Basketball Hall of Fame honours the greatest players and coaches in the game, and captures basketball's excitement, from pro to amateur, and from men to women. Visitors can view rare historic artefacts, play trivia games, watch films and buy souvenirs. There are plenty of interactive exhibits, including the Spalding Shoot Out, where visitors can aim for baskets of different heights from a moving walkway.
1150 West Columbus Ave. Tel: (413) 781 6500. Open: daily 10am–5pm year round. Closed: Thanksgiving, Christmas & New Year's Day. Admission charge.

Nash Dinosaur Land

The Pioneer Valley was inhabited by over a hundred species of dinosaurs 200 million years ago. Geologist Careton Nash discovered dinosaur tracks here 50 years ago, and has excavated extensively in what he calls the largest footprint quarry in the world. There is a small museum and shop adjoining the site.
Route 116, South Hadley. Tel: (413) 467 9566. Open: daily 9am–5pm mid-Apr–mid-Oct; rest of year by appointment. Admission charge.

Six Flags New England

In a suburb called Agawam ('crooked river') is one of the biggest amusement parks in New England. Riverside Park features the Cyclone, one of the country's largest rollercoasters, with more than 50 other exciting rides. The park is also home to many live shows and events, most free to park guests with admission.
1623 Main St, Route 159, Agawam. Tel: (413) 786 9300. www.sixflags.com. Open: daily Jun–Aug 10am–10pm, Sun till 11pm; Sept & Oct weekends only. Admission charge.

Villages

Villages are part and parcel of the New England psyche, as well as the New England landscape. While the terms 'city' and 'town' here refer more to the form of government than to size, a village is simply a grouping of homes, perhaps around a central green, and often with a church or general store. If the village is also the centre of the town's government, there will be a town hall and perhaps a small library.

It is difficult for even non-New England Americans to understand the concept of the village, since it may have a different name entirely from the town it lies in. In fact, a town may have several villages within its political boundaries, each with a different name. In this sense, a New England village is more like a rural form of the city neighbourhood.

What this means to travellers is an endless string of delightful little enclaves, each beckoning a stop for photographs. The quintessential town has a common, a white church with a tall steeple, a general store with a front porch and a cluster of older homes. If the village is on a river or stream, these may include an old stone or brick mill building, now often turned into a store or even a home.

These villages have their historic roots as settlements where groups of families chose to live close to each other for protection and support when they were pioneers carving farms out of the vast wilderness. They built a church, which served as a public meeting house, as well. And from early times they governed themselves at a town meeting. The only state in New England where villages of this sort are rare is Rhode Island, whose history of settlement was not based on the village built around a church. But even here you will find some lovely old villages.

To find these in their most pristine form and heaviest concentration, head for Maine, New Hampshire and Vermont, although you will find them everywhere. Just north of Boston, in the towns around Andover, Ipswich and Boxford, are a number of idyllic clusters, and both western Massachusetts and Connecticut have their share.

Vermont's far northeast corner, the Northeast Kingdom, is well supplied too, as is the Monadnock region of southwestern New Hampshire. Maine's coast has a different sort of highly photogenic village, clustered not around the church, but around a tiny harbour.

Above: Manchester village, Vermont; left: the peace of the town common, Fitzwilliam, New Hampshire

Chesterwood

Stockbridge

This tranquil Berkshire town is graced with a number of historic sites from the Colonial period and the 19th century. Its quaint character was captured by Norman Rockwell, the famed painter who spent the last 25 years of his life here (*see* States of the Arts, *pp132–3*). As in nearby Lenox, the wealthy elite built summer 'cottages' here around the end of the 19th century.

Chesterwood

This was the summer home and studio of monumental sculptor Daniel Chester French. The airy studio still contains clay models and plaster casts for many of his most famous works, including the Lincoln Memorial statue. A railroad track allowed him to roll sculptures outside to view in natural light.
Off Route 183. Tel: (413) 298 3579. Open: May–Oct, daily 10am–5pm. Admission charge.

Naumkeag

Stanford White designed this 23-room mansion in 1886 for New York lawyer Joseph Choate, Ambassador to England (1899–1905). It is an excellent example of the tastes of wealthy families of that era, and the landscaped grounds are particularly fine. In the house is an outstanding collection of Oriental porcelain and ceramics.
Prospect Hill Rd. Tel: (413) 298 3239. Open: late May–mid-Oct, daily 10am–5pm. Admission charge.

Norman Rockwell Museum

This is the world's largest collection of the works of America's best-loved painter of small-town life. His red barn studio, displaying his easel and brushes just as he left them, was moved here from his home. Paintings include the famous *Four Freedoms*.
Main St. Tel: (413) 298 4100. www.nrm.org. Open: Nov–Apr, daily 10am–4pm, weekends 10am–5pm; May–Oct, daily 10am–5pm. Closed: 1 & 18–31 Jan, Thanksgiving & Christmas Day. Admission charge.

Sturbridge

Imagine a typical rural village of the 1830s, spread out over 200 acres with farms, fields and gardens, and you have the recreated village of Old Sturbridge, 58 miles west of Boston. Some buildings were brought to Old Sturbridge from other parts of New England and reconstructed; others are accurate reproductions – both look genuine.

Stop at the Visitor Center for maps, and a 15-minute film on life in an early 19th-century village. Here you will also find the **J Cheney Wells Clock Gallery** (Wells was the founder of Old Sturbridge), which exhibits over a hundred American clocks made by New England clockmakers in the late 18th and early 19th centuries.

From the Visitor Center follow the path to the Common. The guides all wear authentic period clothing down to the shoes, which are made by the village shoemaker. There is also a potter, glassmaker, weaver, printer, blacksmith, cooper and a working sawmill. Meals are served at the Bullard Tavern close to the bridge over the Quinebaug River. *Tel: (508) 347 3362. Open: year-round, but call for seasonal hours. Admission charge.*

Williamstown

Williamstown – a sleepy little town that is one of the most beautiful in all Massachusetts – is synonymous with **Williams College**. The college dates from the late 18th century, and its

elegant buildings are set round spacious lawns. Every summer the highly acclaimed Williamstown Theater Festival (*tel: (413) 597 3399*) takes place opposite, on the college campus, and attracts actors of international repute.

Sterling and Francine Clark Art Institute

One of the finest small art galleries in the country is located here. It has an exceptional collection of works by Picasso, Monet, Renoir and Degas. There are also paintings by American artists, including Winslow Homer and John Singer Sargent, and a small collection of furniture and silver. *225 South St. Tel: (413) 458 2303; www.clarkart.edu. Open: Tue–Sun 10am–5pm. Closed: 1 Jan, Thanksgiving & Christmas Day. Admission charge.*

Naumkeag, Choate family summer residence

Tour: The Mohawk Trail

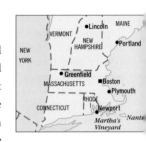

Officially designated Route 2, this road follows an old Pocumtuck Indian trail along the Deerfield and Cold rivers. New England's first scenic road, opened in 1914, it starts in the Connecticut Valley, and finishes in the Berkshire Hills. Many of the sites along its 60-mile stretch date back to the golden age of car touring. Autumn on the Mohawk Trail is particularly spectacular.

Allow 2 hours.

Starting in Greenfield, drive west under Interstate 91. On the right-hand side, soon after heading uphill, there is the Longview Gift Shop and Tower from which, for a nominal fee, you can look out over five states. Continue climbing until the road levels out, passing farms, tiny villages and Indian trading posts. Continue to Shelburne.

1 Gould's Sugar House

Seven miles out of Greenfield, this traditional sugar house still collects maple sap in buckets, and uses a wood fire to boil the sap down to syrup. The best time to visit is during March when the sap is flowing, but the delicious syrup can be tasted all year in the adjoining restaurant.

Continue along Route 2 and take the first left turn into Shelburne Falls.

2 Shelburne Falls

Potholes formed during the last Ice Age

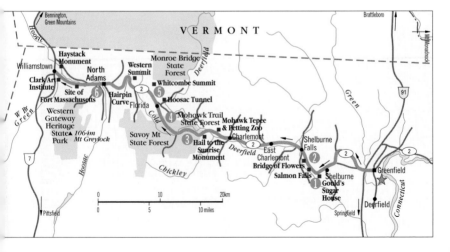

can be seen close to Salmon Falls, on the riverbank near Deerfield Avenue. Also of interest is the Bridge of Flowers, a former trolley bridge that is now an aerial flower garden. Of several good craft shops, North River Glass on Deerfield Avenue, where glass making is demonstrated, is excellent.

Return to Route 2 and turn left. Continue through Charlemont. There are good views of the Deerfield River, and several good picnic stops. On the right is the Mohawk Tepee and Petting Zoo.

3 Hail to the Sunrise Monument

On the left, leaving town, a statue of a Native American raising his hands to the sky stands proudly on a nine-tonne boulder. It was erected in 1932 in honour of the Five Indian Nations of the Mohawk Trail. A pool in front has 100 stones inscribed by tribes and councils from all over America.

Getting more rugged and mountainous, the road narrows and enters a densely wooded area. On the right is a vehicle entrance to the forest.

4 Mohawk Trail State Forest

A bridge over the Deerfield River leads to a fee-paying area with basic recreational facilities including a campground and picnic area. Free parking is available on the right before crossing the bridge, and there are many trails through the forest and along the river that start from here.

Continue up the steep road through beautiful forest scenery. Pass through the village of Florida, with its picturesque church, and continue to Whitcombe Summit.

5 Whitcombe Summit

The lookout tower gives good views of Mount Greylock in Massachusetts, Mount Monadnock in New Hampshire, and the Green Mountains in Vermont. The adjoining motel offers great views from every room.

Continue along the winding road enjoying panoramic views. At Western Summit, look out over the Hoosac Valley; at Hairpin Curve the view stretches from the Hoosac Valley to the Berkshire Valley and the Taconic Range. The road winds steeply down.

6 North Adams

This is an industrial town with several fine red-brick 19th-century mills.

Route 2 continues on to Williamstown and into New York State.

Gould's Sugar House *Mohawk Trail, Shelburne. Tel: (413) 625 6170.*
Mohawk Trail Association *PO Box J, Charlemont, MA 01339.*
Mohawk Trail State Forest *Route 2. Tel: (413) 339 5504.*

Bridge of Flowers, Shelburne

Connecticut

After Massachusetts, Connecticut is the most developed state in New England. It is also the second smallest – only minuscule Rhode Island is smaller. Along the Massachusetts border Connecticut is still very rural, but from Hartford to Long Island Sound the state is much more developed. Connecticut became the most industrialised state in New England, largely because the glacial soil that covers much of the state is just too poor to support crops. Commerce and manufacturing were the means by which the economy grew, and it has become one of the most productive states in the country. Early industries included brass manufacture, firearms (the Colt 45 was developed here), clocks and textiles.

The state of Connecticut was founded by Puritans who felt that Massachusetts was becoming too liberal for their taste. In 1633 they founded three towns by the Connecticut River – Hartford, Wethersfield and Windsor. These were joined together as the Hartford Colony in 1639, and a document called 'The Fundamental Orders of Connecticut' – the world's first written constitution – was drawn up by community elders as a basis for government. Connecticut's nickname, 'The Constitution State', is on every car licence plate of the state today.

Bridgeport

Bridgeport was the home of showman and circus proprietor PT Barnum. In 1891 he willed that a museum be built in the city centre, and the museum is as eccentric as he was. It has three floors of circus memorabilia, including the costumes and furniture belonging to Tom Thumb, a 28-inch-tall man who was Barnum's first major attraction. There is also a 1,000-square-foot model of a three-ring circus, with over 3,000 miniature hand-carved figures.
820 Main St. Tel: (203) 331 9881. Open: Tue–Sat

THE CONNECTICUT VALLEY

This valley follows the longest waterway in New England. A good road follows the river, linking the major sites; alternatively, there are boat trips on the river, including a ferry from Long Island to Haddam.

The Connecticut River Valley and Shoreline Visitors Council (393 Main Street, Middletown, *tel: (800) 486 3346)* is the best place to start, with a mass of information and with detailed maps. There is also an information centre at Westbrook on Route 95.

Route 154 meanders through Old Saybrook, a picturesque town that was the original home of Yale University. It has views over both the Sound, and the mouth of the Connecticut River.

From here the road winds through salt marshes and hugs the river as far as Essex. (Route 9 provides a faster way to Essex.)

10am–4.30pm, Sun from noon.
Closed: holidays. Admission charge.

Chester

Located on Route 154, Chester is
another charming village on the way to
the ferry which crosses to the east bank
of the Connecticut River. The five-
minute crossing operates throughout
the day from April to November at a
nominal charge. Crossing the river, you
will see the silhouette of Gillette Castle
(*see* Hadlyme, *p99*) rising up on the
hillside straight ahead.

East Haddam

At East Haddam, the **Goodspeed Opera
House** has been restored to its former
Victorian glory on the riverbank. It even
has its own dock, which harks back to
Victorian times when many of the
audience arrived by boat. The four-

The Quadrangle at Yale University, New Haven

storey opera house is open for tours;
during the summer, musical revivals are
performed nightly. Also in East Haddam
is a little red schoolhouse where Nathan
Hale taught for two years before he was
hanged as a spy by the British.
Goodspeed Opera House, Route 82.
Tel: (860) 873 8668.

Connecticut

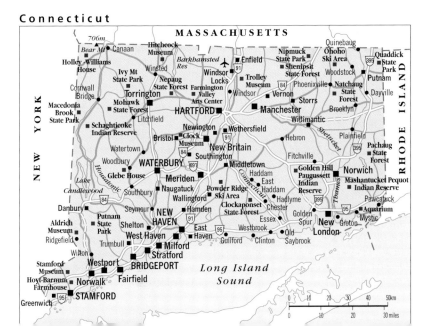

Stone lighthouse, Mystic

Essex

Essex was settled in 1645 and became a major shipbuilding centre. America's first warship, the *Oliver Cromwell*, was built here in 1775. With its tree-lined streets and white clapboard houses, the village has lost none of its old-world charm. On summer weekends it seems that all the boats in Connecticut converge here; a midweek visit is less crowded and more relaxed.

Connecticut River Museum

This has a full-size replica of the first submarine, called the *Turtle*, built in 1775 by a local man. There is also a model of the *Oliver Cromwell*, together with other nautical exhibits.
Main St. Tel: (860) 767 8269. Open: year-round, Tue–Sun 10am–4pm.
Closed: Labor Day, Thanksgiving & Christmas Day. Admission charge.

Steam Train and Riverboat

Follow the Connecticut River Valley in an old-fashioned steam train (first-class available), then connect with an optional riverboat cruise (2 hours total).
Connecticut Valley Railroad, west of exit 3 off Route 9. Open: May–Dec. Admission charge.

Groton and New London

Beside the Thames River lies the US Naval Submarine Base at Groton. Several submersible craft are on display, including the *Turtle*, the world's first prototype submarine. The craft failed to operate successfully, but became the model for submarines of the future. The highlight of the base is the USS *Nautilus*, the world's first nuclear-powered submarine. The *Nautilus* is permanently moored here and is classified as a National Historic Landmark.

Route 12. Tel: (800) 343 0079.
Open: year-round, daily 9am–5pm
(Tue 1–5pm). Closed: Nov–May on Tue.
Free admission.

US Coast Guard Academy

Across the Thames River from Groton, in New London, is the US Coast Guard Academy. It may not sound like a worthwhile place to visit, but do not be deceived – there is plenty of interest, even for landlubbers. The museum has extensive displays on the history of the Coast Guard. The Visitor Center also has displays on Coast Guard history and life as a cadet. The most impressive exhibit, when it is in port, is the *Eagle*, a three-masted, square-rigged training ship built in 1936, which carries cadets to Europe and the Caribbean. It is a beautiful sight sailing out to sea down the Thames.
Mohegan Ave, Route 32, New London.
Tel: (860) 444 8270. Open: Sat 10am–5pm, Sun noon–5pm. Free admission.

Haddam

This little Colonial town, bisected by the Connecticut River, lies on Route 154. Settled in 1662, it was an important fishing and trading port. It is now home to the New England Steamboat Lines, which cruise the Connecticut River and round the coast to Block Island, Martha's Vineyard and Nantucket.

Hadlyme

Although built in 1919, **Gillette Castle**, centrepiece of a state park, looks medieval. Actor-playwright William Gillette became famous portraying Sherlock Holmes, and designed and decorated the idiosyncratic 24-room building. Bedroom mirrors allowed him to see who was downstairs, so that he could decide when to be 'indisposed'.
67 River Rd, Hadlyme. Tel: (860)
526 2336. Open: Jun–mid-Oct, daily
10am–5pm; mid-Oct–Dec, weekends only,
to 4pm. Admission charge.

Goodspeed Opera House, Haddam

Hartford

The high-rise buildings of modern Hartford reflect the importance of trade and commerce to Connecticut's state capital. They also hide the fact that this is one of New England's most historic cities. Originally a Dutch trading post, it became an English settlement in 1635; in 1662 the Colony of Connecticut was established. During the 1700s the city was an important shipbuilding and world trade centre. It later became the insurance capital of the world. Today, Hartford is a pleasant city with just enough history for a short visit.

Mark Twain House

Nook Farm was a neighbourhood in the Hartford suburbs when Mark Twain built his mansion there in 1874. It was here that he wrote most of his best-known works, including *The Adventures of Tom Sawyer* and *The Adventures of Huckleberry Finn*. The house has been skilfully restored and contains a large collection of Twain memorabilia (*tel: (860) 493 6411*).

Next to the Twain House is the home of Harriet Beecher Stowe, author of *Uncle Tom's Cabin*. The house has much of its original furniture, and several paintings by the writer.
351 Farmington Ave. Tel: (860) 525 9317. Open: daily 9.30am–5.30pm, Sun noon–5.30pm. Closed: Jan–May Tue. Admission charge.

Old State House

A Federal-style building designed in 1792 by Charles Bulfinch, this was the first state house in the newly independent United States. The building sits in the downtown district, surrounded by modern office blocks; it was saved from the bulldozer only by the tenacious conservationists. Old State House is home to a museum. The visitor centre inside the building provides free walking maps of the city centre area.
800 Main St. Tel: (860) 522 6766. Open: Mon–Fri 10am–4pm, Sat 11am–4pm. Free admission.

State Capitol

The State Capitol stands prominently above Bushnell Park. It is a classic of Victorian civic architecture, with an interior as flamboyant as the golden-domed exterior.
Capitol information desk and tour guide service, tel: (860) 240 0222.

Wadsworth Atheneum

A short distance from the Old State House is America's oldest public art gallery. The Wadsworth Atheneum houses an excellent eclectic collection of art from Rembrandt and Caravaggio to Willem de Kooning and Frank Stella. Both the French Impressionists and the Hudson School are particularly well represented. There is also a fine collection of early American furniture, tools and household utensils, and the Hammerslough collection of silver.
600 Main St. Tel: (860) 278 2670. Open: Tue–Sun 11am–5pm. Closed: major holidays. Admission charge, but free on Thur.

Litchfield

The town of Litchfield is one of the most attractive Colonial villages in New England. Around a sprawling village green that dates back to 1770 stands a white-steepled church, built in 1829, and houses and shops dating back to the early 1700s. The Litchfield Hills have become a highly fashionable and sought-after weekend holiday address among New York glitterati.

Mystic

During the 19th century, Mystic was one of New England's busiest seaports. Today it is synonymous with **Mystic Seaport**, a recreation of a 19th-century seaport, covering 17 acres of riverfront. There is a children's museum, church, schoolhouse, bank, pharmacy, several shops where craftsmen carve figureheads or work on scrimshaw, a

huge shipyard where wooden sailing ships are worked on, and over 300 ships moored at the village docks, including a wooden whaler. For both the young and old, horse-and-carriage rides and river cruises aboard a steamboat are available. *75 Greenmanville Ave. Tel: (860) 572 5315. Open: daily, spring & autumn 9am–5pm; summer 9am–6pm; winter 10am–4pm. Admission charge.*

Mystic Marinelife Aquarium

This has 48 indoor exhibits, outdoor exhibits of seals, sea lions and penguins, and a 1,400-seat theatre that hosts sea lion, dolphin and whale shows. *Coogan Blvd. Tel: (860) 572 5955. Open: daily 9am–5pm. Admission charge.*

Experience New England's seafaring past in the living maritime museum of Mystic Seaport

New Haven

New Haven is home to one of America's finest universities. Yale is like an oasis in the middle of a neglected 19th-century residential development. The campus of fine old buildings fronting on to green quadrangles proclaims itself to be a venerable academic institution.

Campus tours available through the Visitor Information Center, 14 Elm St. Tel: (203) 432 2300.

Peabody Museum of Natural History

This has an outstanding Hall of Dinosaurs, with a 65-ft brontosaurus skeleton, and zoology, mineralogy and meteorite exhibits.

170 Whitney Ave. Tel: (203) 432 5050. Open: Mon–Sat 10am–5pm, Sun from noon. Closed: major holidays. Admission charge.

Yale Center for British Art

Paintings, drawings, prints, books and sculptures survey British art from Elizabethan times to the present.

1080 Chapel St. Tel: (203) 432 2800. Open: Tue–Sat 10am–5pm, Sun from noon. Closed: major holidays. Free admission.

Yale Collection of Musical Instruments

Over 800 instruments are featured, illustrating 400 years of development. Concerts are held periodically.

15 Hillhouse Ave. Tel: (203) 432 0822. Open: Sept–May, Tue–Thur 1–4pm; Jun, Tue–Thur 1–4pm. Closed: Jul–Aug & major holidays. Free admission.

Yale University Art Gallery

This is the oldest university art museum in the western hemisphere, founded in 1832. It exhibits a variety of classical and contemporary works.

1111 Chapel St. Tel: (203) 432 0600. Open: Tue–Sat 10am–5pm, Sun from 1–6pm. Closed: major holidays. Free admission.

Norwich

The most interesting feature in this small industrial town is the **Leffingwell Inn**. Built in 1675, Thomas Leffingwell bought it in 1770, and opened it as an inn. He subsequently added rooms to extend the inn to its present size. George Washington visited the inn several times during the Revolution, and it has been restored to its appearance at that time.

348 Washington St. Tel: (860) 889 9440. Open: mid-May–mid-Oct, Tue–Sun 2–4pm. Admission charge.

Quiet Corner

The northeast corner of Connecticut seems to have been locked in an earlier age, and its 'Quiet Corner' nickname has certainly been well earned. Few tourists venture into these parts, and there are no towns of any size. The landscape is peaceful and pastoral, but there are a few sites of interest.

Open daily from 9am–5pm is **Caprilands Herb Farm**. It has 31 herb gardens to wander through at no charge, including one that has all the herbs mentioned in Shakespeare's works. *Silver St, Coventry, off Route 44. Tel: (860) 742 7244.*

Roseland Cottage in Woodstock provides one of the finest examples of Gothic Revival architecture.

Route 169. Tel: (860) 928 4074.

Open: Jun–mid-Oct Wed–Sun, 11am–5pm. Admission charge.

Wethersfield

The suburb of Wethersfield, about 10 miles out of Hartford, was one of the original three settlements of the Hartford Colony. Unlike Hartford, Wethersfield retains an extensive historic district, with over 150 houses that predate 1850.

Buttolph-Williams House

Built in 1692, this simple Colonial structure has served as a dwelling house for over 250 years. The interior is complete with period furniture, pewter and 17th-century household items.
249 Broad St. Tel: (860) 529 0460. Open: May–Oct Wed–Mon, 10am–4pm. Closed: Tue. Admission charge.

Webb-Deane-Stevens Museum

Three historic houses have been combined into a single museum which gives a unique opportunity for side-by-side comparison of the lifestyles of three persons with very different characters. All three houses have many original furnishings.
211 Main St. Tel: (860) 529 0612. Open: May–Oct Wed–Mon, 10am–4pm; Nov–Apr Sat–Sun, 10am–4pm. Admission charge.

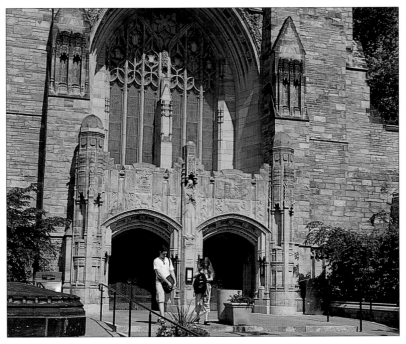

Yale University Library

Maine

Maine was the first part of New England to be discovered by Europeans. In the 11th century the Vikings sailed off these shores, but it was not until 1497 that the Venetian navigator John Cabot claimed the land (inhabited by several Algonquin tribes) for England. The French came in 1604 and, ignoring the English claim, Samuel de Champlain settled an island in the St Croix River. The long and bitter dispute between the British and French was not resolved until 1763. The protracted French and Indian War resulted in the loss of most of the land held by the French in North America.

Portland's Observatory overlooks the harbour

Maine was part of Massachusetts for many years, but it seceded in 1819, and a year later became the 23rd state of the Union. As big as all the other New England states combined, most of its area is covered in pine forests (hence its nickname, the Pine Tree State).

Although the coastline is only 230 miles as the crow flies, it is so rugged and indented that Maine has more linear footage of coastline than any state in the Union – 3,500 miles. In addition, there are over 6,000 lakes and 32,000 miles of winding rivers.

Maine is a wet and wild state that is rightfully described as a vacation paradise (even car licence plates have 'Vacationland' emblazoned across them). Yet it has two distinctly different faces. Most holidaymakers are attracted to the coastline. During the summer, this corridor teems with thousands of people escaping from New York, and even from picturesque Massachusetts, to enjoy this marine paradise.

The other Maine lies in its northern half, a vast area of green wilderness dotted by lakes. This paradise for fishermen, paddlers and hikers has few cities and its towns are widely scattered. Accommodation and facilities for visitors are often clustered around the lakes, especially Moosehead Lake, where facilities range from rustic sporting camps to beautiful inns and lodges with excellent dining rooms.

Autumn is a good time to visit. Maine does not have the same intensity of colour as the mountain states, but at this time of year the heavy summer tourist traffic has left, children are back at school, and Maine is back to its normal, tranquil self. Many of the attractions are only open during the summer, however; most close in the early autumn and reopen the following May, so it is best to check opening times before you visit.

Autumn weather can be spectacular, with warm days and blue skies. Maine winters are often bleak, but there is

Maine

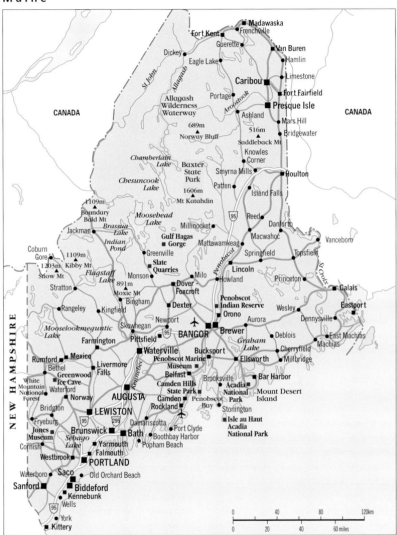

some of the best skiing in the northeast. Spring can be superb, but swarms of black flies and mosquitoes are annoying. Remember that Maine covers a large area. It takes several visits to see it properly, but a short visit to the southern coast should be enough to whet most appetites for more. However, the further north you travel, the more unspoiled and picturesque it becomes.

Acadia National Park

The national park occupies most of **Mount Desert Island**, which was discovered in 1604 by Champlain. There are over 35,000 acres with 170 miles of hiking, biking and horse riding trails. Cadillac Mountain rises to 1,530 feet, the highest point on the eastern coast of the US. The Visitor Center shows a short film on the park, and has free maps and guides. It also has a well-stocked bookstore for the naturalist and the weekly *Beaver Log*, listing the naturalist activities. The park Loop Road (*see box*) passes all the major sites, and even goes to the summit of Cadillac Mountain. The road passes wild, rocky coastline, secluded sandy beaches and thick forests of conifers.

Open: park accessible all year, but Loop Rd closed in winter by snow. Visitor Center. Tel: (207) 288 3338. Open: May–Oct, 8am–6pm (or 4.30pm before 15 Jun & after 15 Oct). Admission charge.

Augusta

Augusta, at the head of navigation on the Kennebec River, has been the state capital since 1832. Before then its main interest was commerce, particularly fur and timber. The city began in 1628 as a fur trading post founded by members of the Plymouth Colony.

Maine State Museum

This museum presents a fascinating and wide-ranging look at Maine's industries and natural environment, with a historical perspective.

State St. Tel: (207) 287 2301. Open: Mon–Fri 9am–5pm, Sat 10am–4pm, Sun 1–4pm. Free admission.

State House

Designed by Boston's Charles Bulfinch and built of local granite, the building has been much extended; it has a graceful portico, and many portraits and battle flags.

State & Capitol Sts. Open: Mon–Fri 8am–4pm. Tours from 9am. Free admission.

Bangor

Today it is a lively small city offering theatres, galleries, a transportation museum, its own baseball team (called the Lumberjacks, of course) and boat cruises on the scenic Penobscot River. Native son Stephen King's home and sites associated with his thrillers are shown on a free map available at Bett's Bookstore.

Chamber of Commerce, 519 Main St. Tel: (207) 947 0307.

Bar Harbor

Bar Harbor, at the entrance of Acadia National Park on Mount Desert Island, has several good shops and galleries, and a very attractive harbour. It became a fashionable summer resort at the turn of the 20th century for wealthy East Coast families, such as the Rockefellers, the Vanderbilts and the Pulitzers. At one time, over 200 mansions overlooked the Atlantic. A disastrous fire in 1947 destroyed most of them; several of those that remain have been converted into inns. The **Bar Harbor Historical Society Museum** documents the town's dazzling past with photographs, newspapers and other memorabilia.

34 Mount Desert St. Tel: (207) 288 4245.

Bath

Bath, 50 miles north of Portland, was a prosperous 19th-century seaport. The town's legacy is preserved in the **Maine Maritime Museum** (*243 Washington St, tel: (207) 443 1316*). In the **Percy and Small Shipyard** there is a collection of small wooden craft used on the coast of Maine in the 19th century. There is also an exhibit on early shipbuilding methods and workshops where apprentices are still learning these time-honoured crafts. From June to October, the *Sherman Zwicker*, a restored schooner, can be visited.
Museum, shipyard and schooner open: daily 9.30am–5pm. Admission charge.

Baxter State Park

The 200,000 acres of land for this park, 85 miles north of Bangor, were purchased by Percival Baxter – twice Governor – for the people of Maine. Baxter willed that this vast tract of prime

forest near the Canadian border be maintained 'forever after in its natural, wild state'. The two highest mountains in the state are located here. Baxter Peak, the 5,267-ft summit of Mount Katahdin, is not only the highest point in the state, but also the end of the 2,000-mile-long Appalachian Trail, which starts in Georgia. This peak catches America's first rays of the sun each morning.

The park is not a place for the casual visitor. Although Route 159 passes through the park, most of the roads are unpaved and facilities are very basic.
Park Headquarters, 64 Balsam Drive, Millinocket. Tel: (207) 723 5140. Open: daily, mid-May–mid-Oct. Admission charge.

The Loop Road on Mount Desert Island gives a 27-mile introduction to all the best sights in the park. For additional information write to the Superintendent, *Acadia National Park, Box 177, Bar Harbor, Maine 04609.*

Nubble Lighthouse, York

Boothbay Harbor

Lying 54 miles northeast of Portland, this town may appear to be the typical, picture-book fishing port for which Maine is famous, but beneath is a full-blown tourist resort – complete with bowling alleys, pinball machines and T-shirts. Take one of the many cruises, fishing trips and excursions on offer at the harbour, including a 90-minute trip to Monhegan Island.

Brunswick

Education is one of the main pursuits of this town, located 25 miles northeast of Portland. At Bowdoin College, founded in 1794, the **Museum of Art** (Walker Art Building) has early American portraits and works by both Winslow Homer and Andrew Wyeth. More unusual is the **Peary-MacMillan Arctic Museum** (Hubbard Hall), which presents the history of polar exploration from ancient times to 1909, when Peary and his assistant MacMillan, both Bowdoin Alumni, became the first to reach the North Pole.
Bowdoin College, Main, Bath and College Sts. Tel: (207) 725 3000; museums: (201) 725 3416. Open: mid-Jun–Aug Tue–Sat, 10am–5pm, Sun 2–5pm; rest of year Tue–Fri 10am–4pm. Free admission.

Freeport

Freeport, 17 miles northeast of Portland, is known as the home of LL Bean, the great American outdoor clothing and equipment supplier, open year round 24 hours a day. Other Freeport cutprice outlets offer the best-known labels at prices far lower than in normal retail shops.

Kennebunkport

Among the more posh of the southern Maine coast towns, Kennebunkport was the centre of attention during the presidency of George Bush Snr, whose ocean-surrounded estate became the Summer White House. Locals became resigned to having their streets blocked by security vehicles, but with the Bush family focus shifting to Texas, the streets of elegant sea captains' homes have resumed their air of genteel quiet.
Chamber of Commerce, 173 Port Rd, Kennebunkport. Tel: (207) 967 0857.

Moosehead Lake

Surrounded by the wilderness that makes up most of northern Maine, sprawling Moosehead Lake offers a variety of outdoor activities. From the town of Greenville, at its southern end, you can take scenic flights in a vintage float-plane, cruise on a restored paddle-wheeler, or watch wildlife from a hired canoe. Fishing and white-water rafting trips are offered by The Birches Resort, *www.birches.com*, with rustic lakeside cabins. Posher accommodation overlooks the lake from Greenville's Lodge at Moosehead Lake, *www.lodgeatmooseheadlake.com*, which also offers packages for fishing and snowmobiling holidays.
Moosehead Lake Chamber of Commerce. Tel: (207) 695 2702.
www.mooseheadlake.org

Old Orchard Beach

For a taste of the old-fashioned fun that once filled New England's beach resort towns, book at The Edgewater, *www.janelle.com*, and revel in Old

Orchard. Miles of very clean beach (locals clean up each day's tourist debris) are punctuated by a pier filled with wonderfully honky-tonk kiosks selling ice cream and fried dough. From the top of the ferris wheel at the pier-side amusement park you can see the whole coast. Finish with fried clams from The Clam Bake, at Pine Point. *Amtrak trains from Boston stop right at the pier; www.oldorchardbeachmaine.com*

Pemaquid Point

The coast of Maine has over 60 lighthouses, but the Pemaquid Lighthouse, 31 miles southeast of Bath, is in one of the most dramatic situations, jutting out on rocky ledges carved by glaciers. The lighthouse is open to the public, with good views of the coast from the top. In the keeper's cottage is a small museum devoted to fishermen, with photographs and artefacts.

Boarding sleighs at the Captain Lord Mansion Inn, Kennebunkport

Fishermen's Museum. Tel: (207) 677 2494. Open: end-May–mid-Oct daily, 10am–5pm, rest of year by appointment. Donations welcome.

Penobscot Bay

The east corner of this huge, island-studded bay forms the western boundary of Acadia National Park. The waters are made for sailing. Tall-masted windjammers and schooners create images from another era as they gracefully navigate the islands.

On the western shore are Rockport and Camden, picturesque towns whose classic harbours overflow with sailing craft and streets are lined by craft galleries and gift shops. Rockland is home to Maine's windjammer sailing ship fleet.

Portland

Although the biggest city in Maine, Portland is still an easy place to explore on foot, and small enough to cover in a very short time. Its hills sweep down to the harbour, and the general atmosphere is one of order and cleanliness. As most people visit Maine for the wild coast and romantic fishing villages, Portland has never suffered from tourist overcrowding. It is a refreshing change to find a major town that is at once unspoiled and worth visiting.

The **Old Port Exchange** on the waterfront is a group of old warehouses that have been renovated and converted into shops, galleries and excellent restaurants. It is a pleasant place to stroll and watch the activity of ferry boats and other maritime traffic around the wharfs. Don't miss the nearby Portland Public Market.

Chamber of Commerce, 60 Pearl St. Tel: (207) 772 2811. Open: daily 9am–5pm.

Portland Museum of Art

This dramatic Post-Modern building, designed by the firm of IM Pei, houses a fine collection of work by notable Maine artists such as Andrew Wyeth, Winslow Homer and Edward Hopper.
7 Congress Square. Tel: (207) 775 6148. Open: May–mid-Oct Sat–Wed, 10am–5pm Thur–Fri 10am–9pm. Closed: Mon mid-Oct–Apr. Admission charge.

Wadsworth Longfellow House

The famous poet Henry Wadsworth Longfellow grew up in Portland, and his childhood home is now a museum. Built by his maternal grandfather, it was the first brick house in Portland.
487 Congress St. Tel: (207) 879 0427. Open: Jun–end-Oct daily, 10am–4pm. Admission charge.

Sabbathday

The **Sabbathday Shaker Community and Museum**, established in 1782 close to Sebago Lake, is one of the oldest Shaker settlements in the United States. Visit the 1794 Meeting House, 1816 Spin House and 1839 Ministry Shop. The buildings have displays of simple but elegant Shaker furniture, textiles and farm tools.
Route 66, New Gloucester. Tel: (207) 926 4597. Open: end-May–mid-Oct Mon–Sat, 10am–4.30pm. Admission charge.

Sebago Lake

Trout and land-locked salmon are Sebago Lake's big attraction for

fishermen. Lakeshore resorts cater for watersports enthusiasts. At its north end, the lake – the second largest in Maine – has fine, sandy beaches ideal for swimming, but they can be overcrowded on summer weekends. Non-aquatic attractions include the Shaker community (*see above*) and the **Jones Museum of Glass and Ceramics**, with over 7,000 items dating from ancient Egypt to the present day.
Jones Museum, Douglas Hill. Tel: (207) 787 3370. Open: mid-May–mid-Nov, Mon–Sat 10am–5pm, Sun 1–5pm. Admission charge.

York

The southern coast of Maine, a two-hour drive from Boston, is the most accessible to visitors. **Kittery**, just south of York, is a centre for discount shopping. Many who flock to beautiful Long Sands Beach, or to photograph the icon, Nubble Light, don't know of York's two other centres.

Millionaires once built summer 'cottages' on the cliffs at York Harbor, and this mini-Newport even has its own Cliff Walk, hugging the sea beneath them. It begins in front of the charming York Harbor Inn (*tel: (202) 363 5119, (800) 343 3869*), with its cosy pub and dining room overlooking the harbour.

Pick up a free walking tour brochure to stroll past the old buildings of historic York Village.

The **Old Gaol Museum** (York Street) opened in 1720 to serve all of Maine. The dark, dank cells are a harsh reminder of the severity of punishment for felons and debtors in the 1800s.

The **Emerson-Wilcox House** (1742)

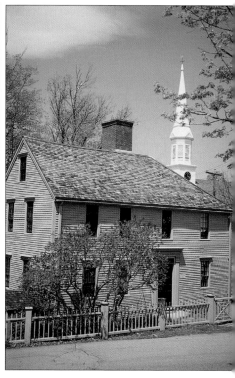

York's historic homes surround its common

has survived many transformations, from tavern to dwelling to tailor's shop to post office. Currently a museum, it has interesting period furnishings. Tours start at Jefferd's Tavern and Schoolhouse. Strong on New England decorative arts, it has the only complete set of 18th-century American crewel bed hangings in existence.
For information on the York Village historical complex, including tours, tel: (207) 363 4974. All the above places are open mid-Jun–Sept Tue–Sat, 10am–5pm, Sun 1–5pm. Closed: Mon. Admission charge.

Rhode Island

With just over 1,200 square miles of land, Rhode Island (short for the State of Rhode Island and Providence Plantations) is the smallest state in the Union. It is divided into east and west by the deeply indented, island-studded Narragansett Bay, which provides some of the best sailing in New England. Altogether, there are 400 miles of coastline in a state that is only 37 miles wide, and it is virtually impossible to find any part of Rhode Island that is more than 25 miles from the sea. Not surprisingly for the undisputed sailing capital of the East Coast, Rhode Island's official nickname is 'The Ocean State'.

Kingscote mansion

Newport

This is one town that no visitor should miss. Like the state of Rhode Island, the town of Newport was settled by free thinkers fleeing from Puritan zealotry. By 1761 Newport was second only to Boston as a port involved in the infamous 'triangle trade', which traded molasses for slaves and then for rum. During the Revolution, the British occupied the town and virtually destroyed it. Yet, even today, Newport's streets are lined with beautifully preserved 18th-century buildings.

Wealthy planters from the Carolinas discovered Newport as a haven from the heat and humidity of the south, and its cool ocean breezes have made this America's sailing capital today. The late 19th and early 20th century was Newport's golden age, when the world's wealthiest families built summer 'cottages' that were equal to the world's great stately homes (*see pp114–15*). John and Jackie Kennedy were married

here, and their wedding reception was held at Hammersmith Farm near Fort Adams State Park. The America's Cup, the world's premier ocean-going yacht race, was held here for 50 years, and the world-renowned Newport Jazz Festival has been a magnet for fans every August for many years.

Today, Newport is a lively, attractive town rising from Narragansett Bay. Its main attraction is a collection of fabulous homes on Bellevue Avenue, which allow the visitor a glimpse of the lifestyle of yesterday's rich and famous. Eight of the most splendid mansions are maintained by the Preservation Society of Newport County (*424 Bellevue Ave, tel: (401) 847 1000*). At any time of year you will find at least two or three of these stately homes are open for tours.

Newport County Convention and Visitors Bureau, 23 America's Cup Ave.
Tel: (401) 845 9123 or (800) 976 5122.
www.GoNewport.com

Rhode Island

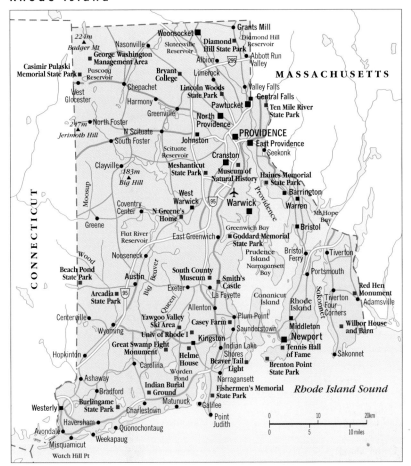

The Astors' Beechwood

The tour here is pure theatre. Costumed actors play the roles of servants, guests and hosts as they guide visitors both above and below stairs.

580 Bellevue Ave. Tel: (401) 846 3772; www.astors-beechwood.com. Open: mid-May–Oct daily 10am–5pm; Nov, daily 10am–4pm; Feb–mid-May, weekends 10am–4pm. Admission charge.

Belcourt Castle

This 60-room Louis XIII-style castle was built in 1891 as the summer residence of Oliver Hazard Perry Belmont. It has the country's largest collection of 13th-century stained glass.

657 Bellevue Ave. Tel: (401) 846 0669. Open: Feb–Mar, Nov–Dec, weekends & holidays 10am–3pm; Apr–Oct, daily 10am–5pm. Admission charge.

The Breakers
Built in 1895, the Breakers is the grandest home in the style of a four-storey Italian Renaissance villa. The 70 rooms are arranged round a great hall, and every surface is embellished by polished or carved marble, mosaics, detailed woodwork, fresco paintings or gold leaf.
Ochre Point Ave. Tel: (401) 847 1000.
Open: Apr–Dec daily, 10am–5pm (till 6pm Sat, Jul–Sept). Admission charge.

Château-sur-Mer
Built in 1852, this building represents one of the best examples of lavish early Victorian architecture in the US.
Bellevue Ave. Tel: (401) 847 1000.
Open: May–Oct daily, 9am–5pm.
Admission charge.

The Elms
This house was built in 1901, modelled on the French Château d'Asnieres. More tasteful than some of its neighbours, The Elms has a restored sunken garden in its landscaped grounds.
Bellevue Ave. Tel: (401) 847 1000.
Open: daily 10am–5pm.
Admission charge.

Hunter House
This is considered to be one of the best examples of Colonial architecture in America. It is open to the public.
54 Washington St. Tel: (401) 847 1000.
Open: Mar–Oct daily, 10am–5pm.
Admission charge.

Kingscote
Kingscote was built in 1839 by Richard Upjohn in a classic early Victorian style. Note particularly the Tiffany windows.

Bellevue Ave. Tel: (401) 847 1000.
Open: May–Oct daily, 10am–5pm.
Admission charge.

Marble House
William Vanderbilt had this sumptuous mansion modelled after the Grand and Petit Trianons in Versailles. An authentic Chinese tea house sits at the end of a lawn overlooking the ocean.
Bellevue Ave. Tel: (401) 847 1000.
Open: late Mar–Dec daily, 10am–5pm.
Admission charge.

Newport Casino
The Newport Casino (1880) is now home to the **International Tennis Hall of Fame** and the Tennis Museum. You can watch court tennis as it was played in the 15th century, and for a fee you can use the grass and indoor courts.
194 Bellevue Ave. Tel: (401) 849 3990.
Open: year-round 9am–5pm.
Admission charge.

Rosecliff
Yet another home modelled after a great French château, it was adapted by the architect Stanford White for Mrs Hermann Oelrichs in 1902. The ball-room is the largest in Newport. It was the scene of many memorable parties.
Bellevue Ave. Tel: (401) 847 1000.
Open: May–Oct daily, 10am–5pm.
Admission charge.

Touro Synagogue
This national historic site was the first Jewish place of worship in North America, built in 1763, and still in use today. The interior is considered an architectural masterpiece.

85 Touro St. Tel: (410) 847 4794. Open: May–Jun Mon–Thur, 1–3pm; Jul–mid-Sept Sun–Fri, 10am–4pm; mid-Sept–15 Oct Mon–Fri, 1–3pm. Free admission.

Wanton-Lyman-Hazard House
This is the oldest restored house in Newport. Built in 1675, it is a fine example of Jacobean architecture and has a restored Colonial garden.
17 Broadway. Tel: (401) 846 0813. www.newporthistorical.org.
Open: by appointment. Admission charge.

Providence
The capital of Rhode Island is New England's third-largest city. Providence does not have the attractions of Newport, but its elegant Benefit Street, known as the 'Mile of History', is quite possibly America's finest textbook of residential architecture, with dozens of examples of Colonial, Federal and Victorian styles. The area includes the State House and the area around Brown University.

Greater Providence Convention and Visitors Bureau, 1 West Exchange St. Tel: (401) 274 1636. Visitor Information Center: Waterplace Park. Tel: (401) 751 1177. www.providencecvb.com

RISD Museum
Part of the Rhode Island School of Design, this outstanding museum contains three floors of artistic treasures spanning several centuries.
224 Benefit St. Tel: (401) 454 6100. Open: Wed–Sun 10am–5pm, Fri 10am–8pm. Closed: New Year's Day, Easter, 4 July, Thanksgiving & Christmas Day. Admission charge, but free on Sat.

Other places to visit include the **Roger Williams Park and Zoo** (1000 Elmwood Avenue, tel: (401) 941 3910); the **State House** (Smith Street, tel: (401) 277 2311); the **John Brown House** (52 Power Street, tel: (401) 331 8575); and the **Providence Athenaeum** (251 Benefit Street, tel: (401) 421 6970).

The Elms

Tour: Newport

This tour through Newport travels through 350 years of history, from pre-Revolutionary days when Newport was a major seaport rivalling Boston, Philadelphia and New York, to the late 1800s – its golden age, when America's wealthiest families built their palatial summer 'cottages' overlooking the ocean. *(See pp112–15 for fuller descriptions of some sites.)*

Allow 1½ hours, longer with visits.

Start at the corner of Long Wharf and America's Cup Ave. Follow America's Cup Ave to Memorial Blvd and turn left into Spring St. Continue to Touro St and turn right.

1 Touro Synagogue
On the left is Touro Synagogue (*see p114*).

2 Newport Historical Society
Next to the synagogue is the Newport Historical Society. The building dates from 1729 and is the oldest Seventh Day Baptist Meeting House in America. In the museum there are displays of period furniture, paintings and rare books.
Continue to Bellevue Ave and turn right. Continue past Memorial Blvd.

3 Newport Casino
On the left is the casino (*see p114*).
Continue a short distance down Bellevue Ave to Bowery St.

4 Kingscote
Kingscote is on the right. This charming cottage was built in 1839 for George

Noble Jones of Georgia and sold to China trader William King in 1864. It still contains the original King family furnishings (*see p114*).
Continue along Bellevue Ave for one block past Perry St.

5 The Elms
On the right is The Elms, built in 1901 for coal magnate Edward Berwind.
Continue and turn left into Narragansett Ave, then right into Ochre Point Ave.

6 The Breakers
The Breakers is on the left opposite Victoria Avenue (*see p114*).
Continue, turn right into Ruggles Ave, then turn left to rejoin Bellevue Ave.

7 Rosecliff
Here, opposite Rovensky Park, is a remarkable concentration of great houses, starting with Rosecliff on the left, and finishing with Belcourt Castle on the right. Among these is Beechwood, home of the Astors. Marble House, Beaulieu, Clarendon Court, Miramar and others (*see pp114–15*).

Follow Bellevue Ave around until it becomes Ocean Ave. Continue to Brenton Point State Park. Ocean Ave eventually becomes Ridge Rd.

8 Hammersmith Farm

On the left is Hammersmith Farm, the childhood summer home of Jackie Onassis. It was here that she and John Kennedy held their wedding reception in 1953. The 28-room mansion was used as Kennedy's 'summer White House'. Close to Hammersmith Farm is President Eisenhower's summer White House, now used by the state for conferences and meetings.
Ridge Rd becomes Harrison Ave.

The Astors' Beechwood

Continue and turn left into Wellington Ave, then right into Thames St, left into Narragansett Ave, and left into Spring St. Follow Spring St to Memorial Blvd, and turn left into America's Cup Ave.

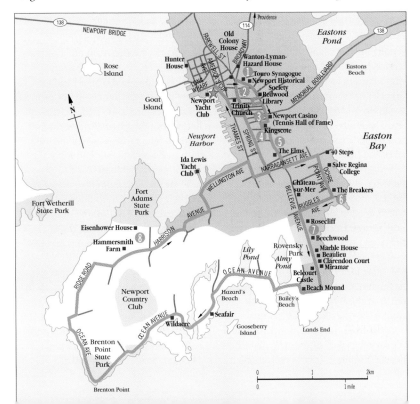

New Hampshire

New Hampshire locals have a reputation for being independent and taciturn, characteristics inherited from their forefathers. It has become a popular place to live in recent years, particularly by commuters to Massachusetts, as it is the only New England state that has neither sales tax nor state income tax.

Daniel Webster statue, Concord

During the Revolution, New Hampshire was the only New England state that was not invaded by the British, and it was the first to declare independence – seven months before the Declaration of Independence.

Between 1623 and 1653, settlements were established along the narrow, 18-mile corridor of coastline. Gradually the settlers moved inland, taming the wild landscape, which includes the highest mountains in New England. One of the beauties of this state is the remarkable variation of scenery in such a relatively small area. The landscape ranges from windswept coast and mountains, to lakes and bucolic villages.

Today, the state is a marriage of industry and wilderness. Its scenic capital, Concord, is not to be confused with Thoreau and Emerson's Concord near Boston (*see pp66–7*). Manchester, the largest town, has a strong 19th-century industrial atmosphere, with red-brick factories and warehouses. At the other extreme are remote hamlets north of the White Mountains that seem to belong in another century.

Apart from the Portsmouth area, it is the northern part of the state that offers the most interest to visitors. Natural beauty and grandeur are the attraction here, rather than historic sites.

Canterbury

Until very recently, two of the last surviving Shakers in New England lived here. The Shakers originally came over from Manchester, England, and established a settlement near Canterbury Center. As in other Shaker communities, they made their own furniture, tools and clothes; and for other necessities they could not produce themselves, they traded medicines and herbs from their organically nurtured gardens. The gardens are still planted with traditional plants, and herbs are on sale in the village shop.

There are 22 buildings in the village, and several are open to the public. Craftsmen still produce the simple and functional wares for which the Shakers were famous, such as brooms and nests of boxes.

Canterbury is worth a visit, even if only for its restaurant serving meals in the traditional Shaker style.
Shaker Rd, off Route 106. Tel: (603) 783 9511. www.shakers.org. Open: May–Oct, daily 10am–5pm. Restaurant open: 11.30am–8pm. Admission charge.

New Hampshire

The Museum of New Hampshire History, Concord

Concord

This has been the capital of New Hampshire since 1808. It is the home of the Concord coach, a high-wheeled wooden carriage that is credited with opening up the wild west. An example of the vehicle, used by Wells Fargo and other stage lines, can be seen at the **Museum of New Hampshire History**. The **Statehouse** is the only one in the nation where the state legislature still meets in the original chambers.

Concord Chamber of Commerce: 244 North Main St, Carrigan Commons. Tel: (603) 224 2508.

Museum of New Hampshire History: 30 Park St. Tel: (603) 228 6688. Open: Tue–Sat 9.30am–5pm. Admission charge.

Statehouse: Main St. Tel: (603) 271 2154. Open: Mon–Fri 8am–4.30pm. Closed: holidays.

Hanover

The Connecticut River Valley has many attractive towns, but none more so than Hanover. The town is synonymous with **Dartmouth College**, the Ivy League institution founded in 1755 by Eleazar Wheelock to spread Christian education among the Native Americans. The campus is one of the most pleasant and beautiful imaginable, its buildings clustered around a beautiful green. Particularly notable is Dartmouth Row, a group of four Greek Revival buildings that exude academic excellence. On the south side of the green, the **Hood Museum of Art** houses ten different galleries; exhibits range from Assyrian reliefs to Picassos. The other important works of art on the campus are frescoes by the Mexican muralist José Clemente Orozco in the **Baker Memorial Library** at the north end of the green.

Hanover Chamber of Commerce: 37 South Main St. Tel: (603) 643 3115. Baker Memorial Library. Tel: (603) 646 2560. Open: daily 8am–midnight; out of term, Mon–Fri 8am–8pm, Sat 9am–6pm, Sun 1–8pm. Free admission.
Hood Museum of Art, Wheelock St. Tel: (603) 646 2808. Open: Tue–Sat 10am–5pm, Sun noon–5pm. Closed: most holidays. Free admission.

Manchester

This town lies 20 miles north of the Massachusetts border on Route 3. Like its English namesake, Manchester has an air of industrialisation. In the 1800s the Amoskeag mills were the biggest textile factory in the world. The old mill building by the Merrimack River still dominates the town. Today, Manchester is the biggest town in New Hampshire, with a population of over 100,000. A site of general interest to visitors is the **Currier Gallery of Art**. The collection concentrates on European and American art from the 13th century to the present, and is considered one of the finest in the United States.
Greater Manchester Chamber of Commerce: 889 Elm St. Tel: (603) 666 6600.
Currier Gallery of Art: 192 Orange St. Tel: (603) 669 6144. www.currier.org. Open: Sun–Thur 11am–5pm, Fri until 9pm, Sat 10am–5pm. Closed: Tue. Admission charge.

Monadnock

The southwestern corner of the state is much more mountainous than the southeast. Each year, more than 100,000 people climb Mount Monadnock, rising to 3,165 feet. Deep in its valleys places like Fitzwilliam, Peterborough, Jaffrey and Keene have everything you associate with New England – white-steepled churches, quiet country roads and covered bridges.

New Hampshire State House, 1819, Concord, New Hampshire

Portsmouth

New Hampshire's only seaport is not just the part of the state most accessible to Boston, but it is also one of the most interesting, with a wealth of historic sites dating back to 1630. This former state capital lies on the banks of the Piscataqua River. In the early 1800s the town was a thriving shipbuilding centre, and its sawmills provided sturdy masts and timber to British shipyards. With the decline of the wooden ship, commerce took over as the main focus of the local economy.

Strawbery Banke

The first settlers in what is now called Portsmouth disembarked after their long sea journey to find the banks of the tidal inlet covered with wild strawberries. From such auspicious beginnings the waterfront settlement of Strawbery Banke developed into a prosperous seaport and centre of commerce. By the 1950s, however, the original historic area was in such a state of decay that it was threatened with 'urban renewal'. Concerned citizens saved it from such a fate by securing federal funds to restore the area. Thirty-eight buildings covering ten acres were spared, and many of them have now been renovated and are open to the public. The restoration project has been done so well that it is hard to believe that Strawbery Banke was ever derelict.

Among the buildings of particular interest are the **First New Hampshire State House** (1758); the **Daniel Webster House**, home of the famous orator and statesman for two years; the **Captain Sherburne House** (1695); the **Captain**

John Wheelwright House (1780), which is perhaps the finest Georgian building here; and the **Captain Keyran Walsh House** (1796), built on a triangular plot so that it has no right-angle corners. Most houses have period furnishings and are open to the public. The gardens of Strawbery Banke are filled with plants of the period, and craftsmen can be found throughout the site, not only using traditional methods in their restoration work but also for making items for sale.

Strawbery Banke Museum: enter off Marcy St. Tel: (603) 433 1100. www.strawberybanke.org. Open: May–Oct, daily 10am–5pm. Closed: Fri in off-season. Admission charge.

Many other fine houses can be found close to Strawbery Banke, and the Greater Portsmouth Chamber of Commerce (*500 Market St, tel: (603) 436 1118, www.portcity.org*) publishes the free *Portsmouth Trail*, a self-guided tour to eight historic homes. Most notable are the **John Paul Jones House**, which has the oldest piano in the United States on display, and the **Governor John Langdon House**, which George Washington visited in 1789.

Most of the houses close during the winter and at other times are only open a few days of the week. Always telephone ahead to confirm opening times.

White Mountains

The White Mountains are the highest range in New England. In the autumn, the vibrant colours of the foliage up here are unsurpassable; in the winter, resorts like Loon Mountain attract skiers from all over the East Coast. The rest of the year it is simply a very beautiful place to be.

The White Mountains Attractions Visitor Center is off I-93 in North Woodstock. Tel: (603) 745 8720 or (800) 346 3687. www.visitwhitemountains.com. Contact this centre to purchase a **White Mountains Attractions Pass** *to 17 destinations at half their usual cost.*

Crawford Notch

A 'notch' is a glacially scarred mountain pass. The Crawfords were a family of 19th-century pioneers in the White Mountains, responsible for cutting the first trail to the summit of Mount Washington. Their cabin in the notch provided shelter for travellers. On the west side of Route 302, driving down from Crawford Notch, a parking area marks the trail head for a one-hour hike up to **Arethusa Falls**.

Just north of Crawford Notch, there is one of the grand hotels of New England, the lavish European-style spa. The **Mount Washington Hotel**, on Route 302 in Bretton Woods (*tel: (603) 278 1000*), has been in operation since 1903. It was the site of the 1944 World Monetary Conference which established an international monetary standard.

The **Mount Washington Cog Railway** departs from the Marshfield Base Station, about six miles east of Bretton Woods (*see* Getting Away, *p141*).

Strawberry Banke, Portsmouth

Franconia Notch

Franconia Notch State Park is one of the great destinations of northern New England, and most of the sights can easily be seen along Interstate 93, the Franconia Notch Parkway. The park headquarters, at the north end of the Parkway, has maps and information on all park activities.

Cannon Mountain is on the west side of the Parkway, and the **Cannon Mountain Aerial Tramway** provides a five-minute gondola ride to the summit – a vertical ascent of over 2,000 feet – for spectacular views over three states and two countries. Cannon Mountain had the first engineered ski slopes in the United States. Appropriately, the **New England Ski Museum** is next door.

Cannon Mountain Aerial Tramway: Franconia Notch Parkway. Tel: (603) 823 5563. www.skimuseum.org. Open: Mid-May–Oct, daily 9am–4.30pm. Admission charge.
New England Ski Museum: Tel: (603) 823 7177. Open: end-May–mid-Oct, daily noon–5pm. Free admission.

Once the most famous landmark in the White Mountains, the **Old Man of the Mountains** was a rock formation high above the lake that was famous for its striking resemblance to a man's profile. Sadly, in May of 2003 the erosion that created the face of rock erased it, and now visitors find more references to the state's favourite landmark than ever before.

The **Basin**, a little further south on the Parkway on the west side, is a huge glacial pothole in the Pemigewasset River. South of this is **The Flume Visitor Center**, which has displays of historic photographs and exhibits of the park. This is also the entrance to **The Flume**, an 800-ft gorge through which flows and falls a brook. A series of stairways leads to the top of The Flume.
The Flume, Franconia Notch Parkway. Tel: (603) 745 8391. Open: late May–late Oct, daily 9am–5pm. Admission charge.

North of Franconia Notch is the village of Franconia. The **Frost Place** is where the poet Robert Frost lived for several years. The simple wooden house is open to the public and contains Frost memorabilia. A Poetry Trail winds through the grounds which inspired some of his best-loved poems.
The Frost Place: off Route 116. Tel: (603) 823 5510. Open: Jun–mid-Oct 1–5pm. Admission charge.

High above Franconia is **Sugar Hill**, a New England classic that is spectacular in the autumn.

Kancamagus Highway

The Kancamagus Highway, from Lincoln to Conway, is one of the great scenic drives in America. In the autumn it is unbeatable (*see pp128–9*).

Mount Washington

Peaking at 6,288 feet, this is the highest mountain east of the Mississippi and north of the Carolinas. It is also one of the most dangerous. The highest wind speed recorded on earth was logged here at an astonishing 231mph. The wind-chill temperatures rival those of the polar regions.

In spite of the often harsh conditions, visitors have an insatiable desire to reach the top. Many go on foot, but a more leisurely ascent can be made by rail. The scenic journey is a three-hour round trip, in a steam train up seemingly impossible grades. An alternative and cheaper, although less romantic, way to reach the top is by the Mount Washington Auto Road. At the top there is a small museum with displays on the geology and wildlife of the area.

Mount Washington Auto Rd, off Route 16, near Gorham. Tel: (603) 466 3988. www.mt-washington.com. Open: daily mid-May–Oct (weather permitting); hours vary, phone for details. Admission charge. Museum open: end-May–3rd week of Oct, daily 8am–8pm. Admission charge (nominal).
Mount Washington Cog Railway: off Route 302, Bretton Woods. Tel: (603) 846 5404. Open: early May–Oct daily. Admission charge.

View from the summit of Mount Washington

New England is synonymous with spectacular autumn colour. Over three million visitors a year come to witness this unrivalled display of nature's beauty in a pastime known as leaf peeping. The colour changes spread down from the far north, usually starting about the middle of September, and peaking in the southern areas of the region by mid-October. The timing and brilliance vary.

The most dramatic colour occurs in the mountain areas of New Hampshire and Vermont. The White Mountains of New Hampshire are reputed to have some of the best fall foliage areas in the world, with over 750,000 acres of uninterrupted forests. The forested slopes of the White Mountains and Vermont's Green Mountains turn to shades of red, orange and yellow almost too bright and breathtaking to be believable.

Events in Vermont are detailed in *Vermont Fall Events* and *Foliage Tours*, available from the Vermont Travel Division (*134 State St, Montpelier, VT 05602, tel: (802) 828 3236*).

Hotlines are provided by each state to give the latest information on leaf-peeping conditions.

Connecticut	(203) 258 4290
Maine	(207) 289 5710
Massachusetts	(617) 727 3201
New Hampshire	(800) 258 3608
Rhode Island	(401) 277 2601
Vermont	(802) 828 3239.

Remember that this is the busiest season for visitors to New England – book well in advance.

Gentle, rolling hills of Vermont's Northeast Kingdom are covered in brilliant foliage and punctuated by white steepled churches, the ultimate New England landscape. Every year in late September the Northeast Kingdom Fall Foliage Festival is held for a week, and Keene, NH's Pumpkin Festival in late October holds the world record for the most carved and lighted jack-o-lanterns, a display that regularly tops 20,000 pumpkins.

Autumn foliage in all its glory, Vermont

Tour: The Kancamagus Highway

The White Mountains of New Hampshire provide some of the most flamboyant autumn colours in the world. This northern section of the Appalachian Trail also provides some of the most beautiful, unspoilt wilderness in all of New England. At any time of year, the Kancamagus Highway will inspire the traveller with its sweeping vistas. The highway connects the Pemigewasset River at Lincoln with the Saco River at Conway. The highway is 34½ miles long and rises to almost 3,000 feet at the Kancamagus Pass.

Start in North Woodstock. There is an excellent visitor information centre here (tel: (603) 745 8720), in addition to a wide range of accommodation and restaurants. Stop at the visitor centre to buy a National Forest parking pass, required for stopping along this route. The most notable sites along the Kancamagus Highway are mentioned here, but there are other lookouts and

picnic areas. Drive east past Loon Mountain Ski Resort for about 11 miles.

1 Pemi Overlook

On the south side of the road, this dramatic overlook gives views of the mountains. Mount Kancamagus is the closest to the lookout, rising to 3,700 feet. *Continue over the pass as the road follows the Swift River.*

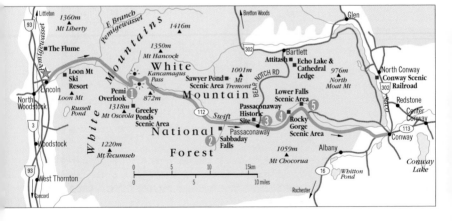

Hiking the Kancamagus' many trails is a popular pastime

2 Sabbaday Falls

A 15-minute walk along the Sabbaday Brook Trail ends at these falls, where the water pours from one huge pothole to another before rushing through a narrow flume.

Continue for 1½ miles to a turn on the left.

3 Passaconaway Historic Site

A self-guiding trail follows the old railway and gives a good introduction to the trees and shrubs of the area. The site is an information and nature centre for White Mountain National Forest. During the summer there are often demonstrations by craftworkers in period costume.

Resume the drive along the highway.

4 Rocky Gorge Scenic Area

The river passes through a narrow canyon at this point, creating rapids that fall into a pool.

5 Lower Falls Scenic Area

The rapids are best viewed from the eastern end of the site. In the summer and autumn these areas can be very crowded, and the best time to visit is midweek.

The drive finishes in the small town of Conway.

Passaconaway Historic Site
Open: end-Jun to Oct, daily 9am–5.30pm. Free admission.

Vermont

The 'Green Mountain State' is aptly nicknamed. Vermont is dotted with hamlets that are every American's dream of idyllic pastoral life. Village greens, white steepled churches and sleepy country lanes combine with mountain scenery and outdoor sports to make this state a holiday paradise.

Bennington is historically important as the site of the Battle of Bennington

Vermont is a state to meander through. Travel slowly and let the countryside work its magic. Virtually every road offers scenery worthy of any calendar. Some of the most memorable and enjoyable experiences will be found by surprise – turning a bend in a country lane to find a picture-perfect village nestled in the woods, chatting with an old country store owner who has lived in the same tiny village for 70 years. The pace of life here is slow.

After their first expedition here in 1609, the French controlled the area for nearly 150 years (the name of the state is derived from the French for green mountain). The British established their first settlement here in 1724 near Brattleboro, but it took another 35 years to defeat the French – and then the colony had to battle with New York over land claims. In 1770 Ethan Allen formed a local militia, the Green Mountain Boys, to protect the new settlers, and with the start of the American Revolution they joined other forces against Britain.

Vermont declared itself an independent state in 1777. It even had its own currency and postal service, and established diplomatic relations with foreign governments. After resolving its difficulties with New York, it became the 14th state of the Union in 1791.

Vermont is the only New England state that does not have a coastline, but it is nevertheless bordered by water. Lake Champlain forms the boundary with New York on the west, and the Connecticut River with New Hampshire on the east. It is the second-largest state in New England, but it has the smallest population. The biggest town – Burlington, on Lake Champlain – has a population of only 40,000.

For those who love the outdoors, Vermont has much to offer all year round. Trails through the Green Mountains are perfect for hiking, and the back roads for cycling. Added to these are windsurfing, canoeing, fishing, golf, skiing, even hot-air ballooning.

Vermont provides an opportunity to get away from it all. At any time of year you can savour the small-town atmosphere of a bygone era. Classic village stores are packed with wheels of cheese, jars of fresh maple syrup and handmade ice cream; in late winter maple sugar houses steam away, producing the delectable amber syrup for which Vermont is famous, and traditional craftsmen welcome visitors to their studios.

Vermont

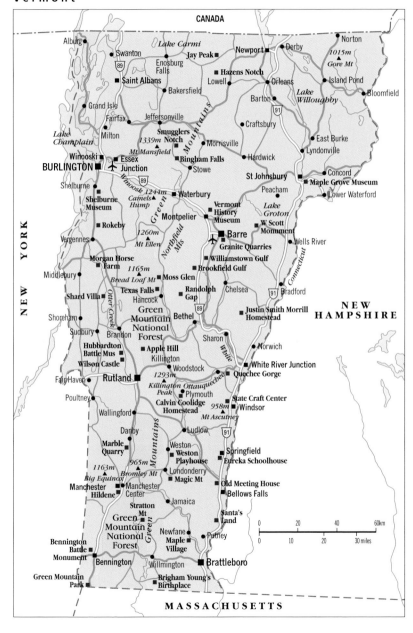

CANADA

Norton

Alburg
Swanton
Lake Carmi
Jay Peak
Newport
Derby
1015m
Gore Mt

Enosburg
Falls
Hazens Notch
Lowell
Orleans
Island Pond
Bloomfield

Saint Albans
Bakersfield
Barton
Lyndonville
Lake
Willoughby

Grand Isle
Fairfax
Jeffersonville
Craftsbury
East Burke

Lake
Champlain
Milton
Smugglers
Notch
1339m
Mt Mansfield
Morrisville
Hardwick
Lyndonville

Winooski
Essex
Junction
Bingham Falls
Stowe
St Johnsbury
Concord
Maple Grove Museum

BURLINGTON
Waterbury
Peacham
Lower Waterford

Shelburne
1244m
Camels
Hump
Vermont
History
Museum
Lake
Groton

Shelburne
Museum
Montpelier
W Scott
Monument

Rokeby
Barre
Wells River

Vergennes
1260m
Mt Ellen
Granite Quarries

Morgan Horse
Farm
Williamstown Gulf

1165m
Bread Loaf Mt
Moss Glen
Brookfield Gulf

Middlebury
Texas Falls
Randolph
Gap
Chelsea
Bradford

Shard Villa
Hancock
Justin Smith Morrill
Homestead

Shoreham
Green
Mountain
National
Forest
Bethel

Sudbury
Brandon
Sharon
Norwich

Hubbardton
Battle Mus
Apple Hill
White
White River Junction

Wilson Castle
Killington
Woodstock
Quechee Gorge

Fair Haven
Rutland
1293m
Killington
Peak
Ottauquechee
Plymouth
State Craft Center
Windsor

Poultney
Calvin Coolidge
Homestead
958m
Mt Ascutney

Wallingford
Ludlow

Danby
Marble
Quarry
Weston
Weston
Playhouse
Springfield
Eureka Schoolhouse

1163m
Big Equinox
965m
Bromley Mt
Londonderry
Magic Mt
Old Meeting House

Manchester
Hildene
Manchester
Center
Bellows Falls

Stratton
Mt
Jamaica

Green
Mountain
National
Forest
Santa's
Land

Bennington
Battle
Monument
Newfane
Maple
Village
Putney

Green Mountain
Park
Bennington
Willmington
Brattleboro

Brigham Young's
Birthplace

NEW YORK

NEW
HAMPSHIRE

Green Mountains

Northfield Mts

Otter Creek

Connecticut

0   20   40   60km
0   10   20   30 miles

MASSACHUSETTS

New England has always been an inspiration to artists, and several painters and sculptors have made New England their home.

Many of the best-known artists of their time produced their major bodies of work in this historic corner of America. John Singleton Copley was the first well-known American portrait painter, closely followed by Gilbert Stuart, whose portraits of George Washington are considered outstanding.

In more recent years, the great illustrator Norman Rockwell lived in Stockbridge, Massachusetts, from 1953 to 1978, producing over 300 covers for the weekly *Saturday Evening Post*. His illustrations of ordinary American family

life came to symbolise the vanishing values of another generation. Many of his former models still live around the Stockbridge area. The only collection of original art by Rockwell can be seen in the Norman Rockwell Museum on Main Street.

In the 19th century Stockbridge was home to America's great monumental sculptor, Daniel Chester French. In his studio at Chesterwood, he produced the working models and plaster casts for the Abraham Lincoln statue that became his most celebrated work. Statues by the prolific sculptor appear all over New England, including the *Minuteman* at Concord and the infamous *John Harvard* statue in Harvard Yard. The studio of the sculptor Augustus Saint-Gaudens is a National Historic Site in Cornish, New Hampshire. Just across the Massachusetts border lies the town of Bennington, Vermont. Anna Moses moved here after growing up a few miles away in New York State. At the age of 76, she took up painting and achieved international fame as one

of the world's great primitives. Grandma Moses lived to be 101, dying in 1961 after 25 productive years. The Bennington Museum has a collection of her works, as well as the table at which she painted, on display in the schoolhouse she attended in Eagle Bridge, New York.

Winslow Homer, and, in more recent years, Andrew Wyeth, worked in Maine during the summer months, producing dramatic paintings of man's relationship with nature.

Facing page above: Art on the Baker Library, Hanover NH;
below: Abraham Lincoln statue
Above: Portland Museum of Art, the Dead Pearl Diver;
right: Saint-Gaudens National Historic Site

Barre

Pronounced 'Bare-ee', this is the home of the largest granite-producing quarries in the United States. The Rock of Ages Company quarry, the world's biggest, is over 350 feet deep and covers 35 acres. For over 150 years Barre granite has been used for the construction of public buildings, but now its major use is for headstones and memorials.

You can visit one of the area's four active quarries in Graniteville, about four miles from the Barre Visitor Information Bureau. Adjacent is the Craftsman Center, where the rough granite is transformed into finished sculpture and monuments.

Rock of Ages: off Route 14, or exit 6 of I-89. Tel: (802) 476 3119; www.rockofages.com. Self-guiding quarry tours: May–Oct Mon–Sat, 8.30am–5pm, Sun noon–5pm; train tours: 1 June–15 Oct Mon–Fri, 9.30am–3.30pm. Admission charge.
Craftsman Center. Open: Mon–Fri 8am–3.30pm. Free admission.

Hope Cemetery to the north of Barre is an outdoor museum dedicated to the stonecarver's art. Headstones, many of them sculpted for the craftsmen's own families, represent the state of the art in monumental stonecarving.
Open: Mon–Fri 7am–4pm.

Bennington

In both 1775 and 1777, Bennington was the centre of action during the American Revolution. The decisive Battle of Bennington is commemorated with a 306-ft high limestone obelisk towering over the town. The top of the

Brattleboro farmers' market

Bennington Battle Monument gives excellent views of the town and neighbouring New York State.

Also in Old Bennington, the **First Church** is one of the most photographed in New England. This Federal-style building, with its original box pews, has six columns, each made from a single pine tree. The cemetery behind the church contains the grave of Robert Frost; the epitaph, which he wrote, reads: 'I had a lover's quarrel with the world'. The nearby **Bennington Museum** is most notable for its collection of the works of Grandma Moses, the great American primitive painter. Her childhood schoolhouse was moved here and reconstructed as part of the museum. The museum also houses Civil War and American Revolution artefacts, a collection of rare blown glass and a fine genealogical library.
First Church: Old Bennington. Tel: (802) 447 1223. Free admission.
Bennington Museum: West Main St. Tel: (802) 447 1571. Open: Mar–Nov daily, 9am–5pm. Admission charge.
Bennington Area Chamber of Commerce is north of town on Route 7. Tel: (802) 447 3311.

Brattleboro

The brick Main Street buildings of this riverside town retain their 19th-century flavour, and the old granite Union Railroad Station houses the **Brattleboro Museum and Art Center**. Locally manufactured Estey parlour organs were found in every prominent household during the 1800s. The museum has several other organs on display, along with other exhibits that keep changing from time to time.

Brattleboro Farmers' Market, Saturday mornings May to October on Route 9, west of town, is rated among New England's best.

Brattleboro Chamber of Commerce: 180 Main St. Tel: (802) 254 4565. Brattleboro Museum and Art Center: Bridge St. Tel: (802) 257 0124. Open: May–Oct, Tue–Sun noon–6pm.

Burlington

Vermont's biggest city rises from the shore of Lake Champlain which, after the Great Lakes, is the largest lake in the United States. It is 150 miles long, and has become an important recreation and holiday resource.

Sightseeing cruises last from 90 minutes, and regular ferries cross New York State, on the western shore of the lake *(for ferry information, tel: (802) 864 9804)*.

The **University of Vermont**, established here in 1791, sits above the town overlooking Lake Champlain from behind green lawns. There is a fine collection of primitive art in the university's **Robert Hull Fleming Museum** on Colchester Avenue *(tel: (802) 656 0750)*.

High-tech industries have been introduced, revitalising the industrial base on which the town was founded.

Lake Champlain Regional Chamber of Commerce: 60 Main St. Tel: (802) 863 3489.

Street fair, Burlington

Jay Peak

Almost at the Canadian border, Jay Peak Ski Resort gets an average of 300 inches of snow a year. Both downhill and cross-country enthusiasts are catered for, but even non-skiers will enjoy a ride on the aerial tramway to the 4,000-foot summit, where there are superlative views of the White Mountains, Lake Champlain, the Adirondacks and into Canada.

Tramway open: late Jun–mid-Oct, daily 10.30am–4.30pm. Admission charge.

Manchester

For more than 150 years, Manchester has been a fashionable resort town. Its elite Equinox House Hotel was once frequented by presidents Taft, Grant and Theodore Roosevelt. Tree-lined, marble pavements surround the Equinox House Historic District. Close to Manchester Center are the popular ski resorts of Stratton, Bromley and Magic Mountain.

American Museum of Fly Fishing

One of America's oldest and most famous fishing tackle manufacturers, Orvis, is based in Manchester, and this museum is close by. Displays of over 3,000 flies and 1,000 rods trace the history of the sport. There are also displays of the tackle belonging to Ernest Hemingway, Dwight Eisenhower, Bing Crosby and other celebrities.

Route 7A, Manchester Village. Tel: (802) 362 3300. Open: daily 10am–4pm. Closed: Thanksgiving, Christmas & New Year's Day. Admission charge.

Robert Todd Lincoln's Hildene

The former home of Abraham Lincoln's son Robert sits in 412 landscaped acres two miles south of town. The 24-room Gothic Revival mansion was built in 1905 as a summer home for Lincoln, who at the time was chairman of the Pullman Car Company. The house is now a museum full of period furnishings.

The Equinox Hotel & Resort, Manchester

Country church near Plymouth

Route 7A, Manchester Village. Tel: (802) 362 1788. Open: mid-May–Oct, daily 9.30am–4pm. Admission charge.

Montpelier

The nation's smallest state capital is dominated by the gleaming, golden dome of the State House, which was modelled after the Temple of Theseus in Greece. Although this is a very pleasant city cradled in wooded hillsides, there is not very much to interest the visitor except good restaurants.

Vermont Travel Department, 134 State St. Tel: (802) 828 3236/(800) VERMONT. www.1-800-vermont.com

Northeast Kingdom

For lovers of peace, solitude and wide-open spaces, this is the area to visit. **St Johnsbury** is the commercial and cultural centre of the region. The **Maple Grove Museum**, with a candy factory and house, gives a good introduction to the production of maple syrup. However, up here in the far north it is the tiny hamlets and rolling hillsides that are of more interest. Mile upon mile of forests, lakes and valleys are punctuated by the occasional postcard village. When the leaves turn, the Northeast Kingdom Annual Foliage Festival offers flea markets, pancake breakfasts, harvest activities and other events, usually at the end of September and beginning of October.

Details from the Northeast Kingdom Chamber of Commerce. Tel: (802) 748 3678 or (800) 639 6379.

Peacham

Peacham (*21 miles southwest of St Johnsbury, on Route 15*) is perhaps the most picturesque of the Northeast Kingdom villages, with its white houses, steepled church and academy.

It is one of the most photographed during the foliage season. A classic general store has just about everything that the population of 611 could need.

Plymouth

Plymouth (*6 miles south of Route 4 on Route 100*) was the birthplace of Calvin Coolidge, the 30th president of the United States. The **Coolidge Homestead** and **Coolidge Birthplace** are open to the public and the farm includes a working creamery, where Vermont cheddar is still made. Here you can also find other historic buildings.

Quechee Gorge

Not far from Woodstock, Route 4 crosses a high bridge. Stop, walk, and look over the edge into the immense rocky chasm carved out by the Ottauquechee River during the Ice Age. It is a one-mile walk to the bottom of the 165-foot deep gorge, known as 'Vermont's Little Grand Canyon'.

Rutland

Vermont's second-largest town was an important centre for quarrying marble; 250,000 headstones at Arlington National Cemetery in Virginia came from here, as did the marble for the Lincoln Memorial in Washington. The **Vermont Marble Company Exhibit** (*61 Main St, tel: (802) 459 3311*) explains the history of the industry with a series of descriptive displays.

Shelburne

One of the biggest attractions in the state is the **Shelburne Museum**, with 37 buildings covering 45 acres. Paintings and other fine art are only the beginning of the 80,000-artefact collection. You'll see American pieced quilts, carved decoys, carousel horses, sleighs and historical houses filled with furniture – in short, three centuries of Americana. *Tel: (802) 985 3346. Open: mid-May–mid-Oct, 10am–5pm; shorter winter hours. Admission charge.*

Shelburne Farms was part of the estate of Dr William Seward Webb and his wife, Lila Vanderbilt Webb. It is still in operation as a learning centre, and includes a working dairy farm and a cheese factory. The Queen Anne Revival house operates as an inn. Covered-wagon tours of the 1,000-acre estate and other events are offered throughout the summer. *Tel: (802) 985 8686. www.shelburnemuseum.org. Tours: mid-May–Oct, 10am–5pm. Admission charge.*

Stowe

Stowe, with over 60 miles of cross-country ski and hiking trails, was the home of the famous Von Trapp family immortalised by *The Sound of Music*; the countryside reminded them of their native Austria. The **Trapp Family Lodge**, off Route 108, is a popular resort visited all year round.

Woodstock

This elegant town of well-preserved Federal-style houses has a large and attractive village green, an old, covered bridge and four church bells that were made by Paul Revere. The **Billings Farm and Museum** is a working dairy farm showing life on an 1890s farm. Frederick Billings, father-in-law of John D Rockefeller, made his money in railroads, but his interest was in animal husbandry and conservation. *Tel: (802) 457 2355. Open: May–Oct 9am–5pm. Admission charge.*

The buildings of Woodstock are beautifully preserved

Getting Away From it All

Although driving at a relaxed pace through the states is pleasurable enough, more exciting possibilities exist through activities such as whale-watching, canoeing or kayaking, or hiking up the Appalachian Trail.

Country lane, Vermont

Sylvan Solitude

Thirty minutes from downtown Boston, on Jamaica Plain, there are over 7,000 different species of trees and shrubs, and hardly any people. The **Arnold Arboretum** of Harvard University started as a tree farm in 1872, and now plants and trees from around the world fill its 265 acres. The park is particularly spectacular during May and June, when many of the specimens are in full bloom. There are a number of paths through the arboretum, offering walks of up to an hour in length.

125 Arborway, Jamaica Plain.
Tel: (617) 524 1718. Open: daily from sunrise to sunset. Free admission.

A Grave Affair

Mount Auburn Cemetery in Cambridge (1831) was the first cemetery in the United States to be landscaped, and changed the way cemeteries were to look from then on. This 170-acre botanical garden, complete with lakes and bridges, is also the resting place for many of Cambridge's and Boston's most notable figures. Henry Wadsworth Longfellow lies here, along with jurist Oliver Wendell Holmes, architect Charles Bulfinch, suffragist Julia Ward Howe and Mary Baker Eddy, the founder of the Christian Science Church.

580 Mount Auburn St, Cambridge. Tel: (617) 547 7105. Open: daily until dusk.

Blue Hills Reservation

This 7,000-acre park south of Boston is a vast recreational playground below the highest point in eastern Massachusetts. The Great Blue Hill is the site of a lookout and the oldest weather station in North America. Dozens of hills are covered with forest, and sheltering lakes are filled with trout, bass, bullhead, perch and sunfish. There are over 500 miles of hiking, biking, bridle and cross-country ski trails. Other facilities include ice-skating rinks, tennis courts, a golf course and even a downhill ski run. The **Trailside Museum** is a natural history museum with live animals, and the 1795 **Redman Farmhouse** is among the 16 historic sites.

Reservation Headquarters: 695 Hillside St, Milton. Tel: (617) 698 1802. Open: Tue–Sun, but car parks open daily from dawn to dusk. Free admission.
Trailside Museum: Tel: (617) 333 0690. Open: Tue–Sat 10am–5pm, also Mon during holidays. Admission charge.

Wet and Wild

Belle Isle Marsh is the last extensive area of saltmarsh remaining in the city of Boston. In the 1630s it was grazing land

for sheep, but now it is wild marsh set off by the unusual backdrop of the Boston skyline. There are walkways throughout the marsh; don't be surprised if you are the only person exploring them.
To get there, take the T to Suffolk Downs Station.

Watching Whales

Whales cruise off the New England coast from April to November, gathering at

Franconia Notch and Profile Lake from Cannon Mountain

the major feeding grounds off the Massachusetts coast, Jeffery's Ledge and the Stellwagen Bank. These huge mammals reach up to 70 feet in length. Even a fleeting glimpse is a thrilling experience. Among the species that can be seen are the finback, the humpback, minkes and the right whales.

Whale-watching cruises operate out of most of the major seaports, including Gloucester and Provincetown on Cape Cod and Portsmouth, New Hampshire. In Boston, cruises are operated by several companies, including: **New England Aquarium** (*tel: (617) 542 8000*), **AC Cruise Lines** (*tel: (617) 261 6633*), and **Bay State Provincetown Cruise** (*tel: (617) 748 1428*).

Letting off Steam

Steam engines are alive and well in New England. The world's first mountain-climbing locomotive was 'Old Pepperass', which reached the summit of Mount Washington on 3 July 1869. The engine is now on display at the base station for New Hampshire's **Mount Washington**

Cog Railway, which is still the only cog railway in the world entirely powered by steam. It takes 2 tonnes of coal and 2,000 gallons of water to push one carriage to the top of the mountain. The 3-mile journey, which takes three hours, is the second-steepest railway track in the world. The train operates from early May to October.
Off Route 302, Bretton Woods, NH. Tel: (603) 278 5404 or (800) 922 8825. www.thecog.com

Down on the Mount Washington Valley floor, the **Conway Scenic Railroad** takes passengers on a journey back in time in both open and closed restored carriages. A one-hour ride covers 11 miles, and finishes at the 1874 depot, which has a small museum. A dining car has recently been added, making the ride even more enjoyable. Longer trips are occasionally made through Crawford Notch.
Route 16, North Conway, NH. Tel: (603) 356 5251. www.conwayscenic.com. Open: mid-Apr–mid-Dec.

Step back into the 19th century at Old Sturbridge Village

In Connecticut, the **Valley Railroad** winds for an hour up the beautiful Connecticut River Valley from Essex to Chester using a 1920 steam engine and rolling stock. A delightful variation on the trip is to disembark at Deep River and take a leisurely riverboat journey back to Essex (*see p98*).
Railroad Ave, Essex. Tel: (203) 767 0103. Open: May–Dec. Telephone for times.

The **Berkshire Scenic Railway** in Lenox, Massachusetts, runs only diesel engines, but the ride will delight the railway enthusiast. As the railway is run by volunteers on a very irregular basis, it is always essential to telephone for schedules. There is an interesting collection of memorabilia at the Lenox depot.
Housatonic St, off Route 7 (Lenox Bypass). Tel: (413) 637 2210. Open: May–Nov weekends.

Looking at Lakes
Lake Winnipesaukee, covering 72 square miles, is the largest lake in New Hampshire. It is surrounded by three mountain ranges and has 365 islands. Native Americans called it 'the beautiful water in a high place', and the best way to experience it is aboard the MS *Mount Washington.* During the summer this 230-ft passenger steamship gives daily 50-mile, 3¼-hour cruises of the lake as well as evening theme cruises; every Sunday during the season there is a champagne brunch cruise.
Departs from Weirs Beach daily, May–Oct. Tel: (603) 366 2628.

A more original way to see the area is aboard the MV *Sophie C* mail boat, which delivers the post to summer residents of the islands in the northern part of the lake. This is the country's first floating post office, established in 1892.
Departs from Weirs Beach daily in May, Jun & Sept at 1.30pm; during Jul & Aug, daily at 11am–1.30pm. Tel: (603) 366 5531.

On **Lake Champlain** in Vermont, throughout the summer, there are several daily ferries that make the one-hour crossing from Burlington to Port Kent in New York State, providing an inexpensive way to enjoy the scenery.

Island Hopping
The coast of New England is scattered with islands. Some are major resorts like

Martha's Vineyard, while many are just rocks sticking out of the sea. But there are a few that allow the ideal escape away from the crowds.

In Boston Harbor there are over 30 islands. Some have been joined to the mainland, one group became Logan Airport, and several were once used for housing prisoners or soldiers. **Georges Island** is the site of Fort Warren, built in the mid-1800s. It was used as a prison for Confederate soldiers during the Civil War, and since then it has been left more or less undisturbed. It is also the headquarters for the **Boston Harbor Islands State Park**, which covers seven islands in the bay. The ferry to Georges Island from Long Wharf in Boston takes about 45 minutes. During the summer, free water taxis serve **Gallops, Lovells, Peddocks, Bumpkin** and **Grape Islands**. On **Little Brewster**, the most remote island, stands the **Boston Light**, the oldest lighthouse in the country. The original lighthouse, built in 1716, was blown up by the British in 1776; the present building was constructed in 1782.

All of the islands give great views of the Boston skyline, and some of them have basic camping facilities.

Several organisations operate boat services to the islands: **Boston Harbor Explorers** (*tel: (617) 479 1871*) offers cruises to the more remote islands. Others are: **Boston Harbor Cruises** (*tel: (617) 487 4602*), **Boston Harbor Commuter** (*tel: (617) 740 1253*) and **Bay State Cruises** (*tel: (617) 748 1428*).

The worn cliffs, Block Island

Block Island

Lying 12 miles south of Newport, Block Island is Rhode Island's answer to Nantucket and Martha's Vineyard – without the glitter. Several ferries operate daily from Point Judith, and the crossing takes an hour. During the summer, there are also ferries from Providence, Newport, New London, Connecticut and Montauk, Long Island. All the ferries usually have space available unless you are travelling with a car. Block Island is only seven miles long and three miles wide and ideally suited to discovery by hired bicycle or moped. Mopeds are restricted on some of the smaller dirt roads, so bicycles are really the best way to travel around.

The island is relatively undeveloped and facilities are deliberately limited. During the summer, accommodation is

'Thar she blows!' – that familiar refrain shouted from the crow's nest of a ship by a sailor on watch – was the call to action for whaling, one of 19th-century New England's most important industries. Referring to the misty spray a whale emits when surfacing to breathe, the sailor's cry signalled an era of prosperity for New England that lasted for over a century.

Captured in Herman Melville's novel *Moby Dick*, whaling was a hard life that carried great risks – and riches. Whale oil was used to light streets and homes in the United States and Europe

during much of the 18th and 19th centuries. The main suppliers were the hundreds of ships based in Nantucket and New Bedford that scoured the oceans from Greenland to Polynesia. Three-masted whale ships carried a crew of 15 to 20 on trips that kept men on the open waters for months at a time. The hunt began when harpooners on small rowing boats would hurl their weapons at an area just behind the animal's eye. Harpooned whales would then either dive, attack the boat or flee, pulling the boat along in what was known as a 'Nantucket sleigh ride'. Eventually, the whale would succumb to a series of carefully placed spears, and the processing of whale oil, meat and other whale products would begin on board the ship.

With the discovery of petroleum in 1859, whaling began a precipitous decline. While this type of whaling did deplete populations, it was the advent of mega-ship modern whaling fleets that seriously endangered the whale. Today, whaling is banned in the United States, yet the cry of 'thar she blows' can still be heard aboard ships that take adventurous visitors on whale-watching trips from early summer to late October. In Provincetown, try Dolphin Fleet (*tel: (508) 240 3636*) or Whale Watcher (*tel: (508) 362 6088*); several other companies also offer trips along the North Shore of Massachusetts and the Maine coast.

Facing page: a whale breaching; below: close encounter with a giant – humpbacks can reach 40 to 50 feet and weigh 30 tons

booked solid for months ahead, so plans must be made well in advance.

Old Harbor is the first settlement you see on the island. A tourist boom early last century resulted in a number of grand hotels and restaurants being built there. From here a good paved road circles the island, leading to many pristine beaches and natural history trails. The interior of the island is grassy moorland. South of Old Harbor is the Southeast Point Light, close to the spectacular, multicoloured, 200-ft cliffs of **Mohegan Bluffs**. At the northern end of the island is a bird and wildlife refuge called **Sandy Point**.

Monhegan Island

There is a profusion of islands off the coast of Maine, but Monhegan Island is a perennial favourite. The ferry to the island, a mail boat called *Laura B*, leaves from Port Clyde, 9 miles away on the mid-Maine coast (twice daily during summer, reservations essential). The short crossing transports visitors to another century. Monhegan Island was settled in 1720 and has not changed much since then. There is still no electricity, few inhabitants, and therefore few vehicles. Lobster-fishing is the only industry on the island, although a small artists' community has been attracted by the location.

Saltwater Sailing

Newport has long been considered America's sailing capital, so where better could one learn to sail? **America's Cup Charters** takes passengers on legendary winners of the world's greatest yacht

race, with the world's largest and classic Twelve-Metre fleet (*tel: charters (401) 849 5868; sunset sails (401) 846 9886; www.americascupcharters.com*).

To handle a sailing boat yourself, learn the ropes with **Sail Newport** who provide professional instruction for all ages and skill levels. (*Fort Adams State Park, tel: (401) 849 8385; www.sailnewport.org*)

Sporting Opportunities
Cycling

With its winding roads, irregular terrain and scenic small towns, New England has drawn bicycle-touring enthusiasts from across America and around the world. In Boston, pedal on the Dr Paul Dudley White Bike Path, a 25-mile loop that takes you from the Science Park to Watertown Square along the historic Charles River. Visitors to Vermont can enjoy wonderful tours of country towns on their own or with **Vermont Bicycle Touring** (*tel: (808) 453 4811*), one of several cycling companies that offer weekend or longer tours in the region.

Hiking

The Appalachian Trail, one of the best-maintained hiking routes in America, runs the length of New England, up pristine mountain ridges and through lush valleys. The five-mile hike up the region's tallest peak, 6,288-ft Mount Washington in New Hampshire, gives a sense of the diversity of New England flora and fauna. The trek takes you from deciduous forest to Arctic tundra, the botanical equivalent of travelling 600 miles north to the Canadian wilderness. The **Appalachian Mountain Club** (*tel: (603) 466 2727*) maintains trails and a string of huts along the trail, and can offer assistance in planning a trip or reserving a hut.

Canoeing/Kayaking

With lakes and ponds in each of the six states, rivers and a coastline marked by beautiful bays and estuaries, New England offers a lifetime of paddling opportunities. The Androscoggin and Saco Rivers in New Hampshire and Maine are favourites for white water, and nearly every lake and pond must have at least one public access point for paddlers. LL Bean, in Freeport, Maine, operates an outstanding learning centre for sea kayaking (*tel: (888) 552-3261*). *For details of other sports, see* pp158–61.

Autumn on a New England pond

Shopping

New England is a shopper's dream. Not only can you find anything and everything, but the prices are attractive, too.

What to Buy

Books

The streets around Harvard Square in Cambridge, Massachusetts, have America's highest concentration of bookstores, many of which carry second-hand volumes at tremendous savings. **Harvard Bookstore** at 1256 Massachusetts Avenue is the best. Another good one is **Starr Book Shop** at 29 Plympton Street. Museum shops are an excellent source of books on specialised subjects such as art, history and culture. Look here, too, for high-quality gifts, jewellery and souvenirs, most often authentic reproductions of pieces in the museum. Especially good shops are at Boston's Science Museum and Museum of Fine Arts, the Preservation Society of Newport County

Craft shows are a good place to find handmade items

(Rhode Island) and Old Sturbridge Village (Massachusetts).

Clothes

Clothes are available in a wide variety of styles and prices, from French designer dresses and Savile Row suits to denim jeans. For the height of fashion and designs from the couture houses, there is no shortage of shops. Boston's **Newbury Street** is full of them – but don't expect a bargain.

Neiman Marcus, **Nordstrom** and **Sak's Fifth Avenue** have designer clothes and recognised name brands. Frequent sales offer good savings and are advertised in local newspapers.

The best buys in New England are to be found in the basement of **Filene's**, a department store in Boston's Downtown Crossing. It is full of incredible bargains with prices often as low as 10 per cent of the original price. Outlet stores, operated by manufacturers, feature seconds and discontinued lines at very low prices. Some of the best, including **Ralph Lauren's Polo Shop** and **LL Bean** (a mail-order outdoor clothing and equipment supplier), are in Freeport, Maine. Other good outlet centres are Kittery, Maine; Manchester, Vermont; and Conway, New Hampshire.

Electrical Goods

All mains-powered equipment is for 110 volts at 60 cycles, but battery-powered gadgets use international battery sizes, and are often an excellent buy. As one of the major centres of America's high-tech industry, Boston has plenty of computer peripherals and software at bargain prices. Determine compatibility with overseas systems first.

Photographic Equipment

The US is currently one of the cheapest places in the world to buy cameras and lenses, but always check on the lowest prices first. *Popular Photography*, a monthly magazine, carries dozens of ads for discounted equipment. These are usually in New York, but give an idea of a reasonable price range. Many shops will negotiate rather than lose a sale.

Cameras sold in the US frequently have a designation different from the rest of the world. The Nikon 8008 is identical to the Nikon 801, but the shop assistants may not know this. Check on the specifications before you leave home. Remember, too, that the US designations are obvious to customs officials.

Film of all makes, types and formats is widely available at very low prices.

Souvenirs

Perennially popular, maple syrup is sold in quaint tin containers. Museum shops generally have very high-quality merchandise, which is frequently educational. Crafts range from pottery to scrimshaw, and are easily found in craft galleries and craft fairs, common throughout the region. New England is one of the few places in America with an abundance of antique shops. There are some very fine pieces to be found, but few bargains. Some of the best places for antiquing are in the Berkshires of western Massachusetts, Cape Cod (particularly along Route 6A and in Chatham), Connecticut's Litchfield County and Newport, Rhode Island.

Where to Buy
BOSTON

Boylston Street
Boylston runs parallel to Newbury Street just one block away. The Ritz-Carlton Hotel, probably Boston's finest, is just off one end of Boylston Street. Across the street next to the Ritz Parking Garage is **Firestone and Parson**, one of the city's best jewellery stores. Around the corner is **Shreve, Crump and Low**, a favourite old New England jewellery store which also sells antique silver and porcelain. You can get posh clothes at bargain prices at Marshall's without leaving Boylston Street, or step over to Hermes for the extravagant side.

Charles Street
From the corner of Boston Common and the Public Garden to Cambridge Street, Charles Street is a paradise for antique hunters. Dozens of small shops in basements, on second floors and down alleys offer an eclectic range of old things, from genuine, fine antiques to yesterday's ephemera.

Copley Place
This glitzy shopping mall, together with The Shops on the Pru, at the corner of Copley Square in Back Bay, houses 100 of the most elegant and expensive stores in Boston. The main tenant is **Neiman Marcus**, with neighbours such as **Tiffany**, **Gucci**, **Louis Vuitton** and **Bally** of Switzerland. The centre also houses the newly opened **Barney's NY**, and several good restaurants.

Downtown Crossing
This is the heart of the central shopping district, anchored by two department stores, **Filene's** and **Macy's**, the biggest department store in New England.

Downtown Crossing is a pedestrian zone, and there are always lots of hawkers selling from pushcarts. Apart from the two main stores, there are several excellent jewellery stores close by.

Faneuil Hall Marketplace
Since opening in 1976, 20 million people a year have visited this shopping area, which has become Boston's number-one tourist attraction. This is not the place to look for elegance or sophistication, however. Most of the shops found here are popular chain stores, such as the **Body Shop** and **Crate & Barrell**, although there are some worthwhile souvenirs to be found.

Newbury Street
Without a doubt, this is the trendiest, classiest and most elegant shopping street in New England. Once making up an exclusive residential street in Back Bay, the brownstone houses are now home to **Brooks Brothers**, **Cartier**, **Burberry** and a host of other fine stores, including **Louis**, which is the most chic men's store in town.

Newbury Street has more art galleries than any other stretch of road in America, but most of them are on upper floors, so remember to look up. Sidewalk (pavement) cafés are interspersed with the elegant shops, giving the street a very European flavour. Newbury Street ends with a gigantic **Virgin Records** store. Music from all over the world is found here, and it is possible to satisfy the most esoteric musical tastes.

Quincy Market

The Quincy Market building is full of food stalls, the Bull Market has pushcarts loaded with souvenirs and crafts, and the North and South Markets have a more traditional range of clothes shops. Here, too, you will find **Banana Republic**, which was originally an army surplus store, but developed into a casual clothing store.

CAMBRIDGE
CambridgeSide

This is the region's newest shopping complex. The main tenants are **Filene's** (without the basement!) and **Sears**. Many of the smaller shops are more interesting, and include the upmarket clothiers **Abercrombie and Fitch**.

Harvard Square

Harvard Square is the most popular hang-out spot in Cambridge, where students and tourists alike frequent the shops and pavements to enjoy a range of cultural happenings. Some prefer to sit and listen to street musicians (it is here that Tracy Chapman got her start) and others pass their time at Au Bon Pain playing chess or hypothesising over coffee and overpriced baked goods.

Whatever the interests, the square is the best place to find any Harvard-insignia souvenirs, and there are many other fascinating shops in the vicinity including the terminally 'hip' **Urban Outfitters** and perhaps the most organic cosmetics found at **Origins**.

Shoppers on Charles Street, Boston

Entertainment

Boston and Cambridge are, without doubt, the entertainment capitals of New England. Other cities have theatre, music and dance, but none can match the range or professionalism of Boston and Cambridge.

Common Ground Fair, Unity, Maine

Both London's West End and Broadway shows are featured at theatres in Boston, complemented by a multitude of small theatres producing both experimental and traditional drama. The comedy clubs here rank with metropolitan New York and Los Angeles.

Music fans are well catered for, not only with an acoustically perfect Symphony Hall, but also with the outstanding Boston Symphony Orchestra, the renowned Boston Pops Orchestra, numerous jazz clubs, one of the great American folk clubs and a host of rock clubs. Although Boston has never been a particularly wild town at night, in recent years a number of establishments have

Summer theatre and opera are found all over New England

The Hatch Shell on the Esplanade, venue for summer concerts

emerged that make a dent in this staid image.

For details of current offerings, the best source of information is either the Thursday 'Calendar' section of the *Boston Globe*, the weekly *Boston Phoenix*, published every Friday, or *Where Boston*, published monthly. **Boston by Phone** is a 24-hour telephone information service. Dial *(888) SEE-BOSTON* and listen to the menu of options for access to detailed

information (the website for **Greater Boston Convention and Visitors Bureau** is at *www.bostonusa.com*). For up-to-the-minute details of current events, try the *Boston Globe* (*www.boston.com*).

All year round, events take place throughout New England, from county fairs to film and jazz festivals. The dates and venues are different every year, but the various state offices of tourism will be able to provide information.

A lively party at The Astors' Beechwood

Tickets can usually be purchased at the venue, on the telephone by credit card, or through a computerised ticket service by phone with a credit card. One of the biggest is **Ticketmaster** (*tel: (617) 931 2000*). There is also **Ace Ticket Agency** (*tel: (617) 734 6666*). Agencies usually add a service charge to the ticket price.

Day-of-performance tickets can be bought at half price from **Bostix**, with ticket booths at Faneuil Hall Marketplace and Copley Square opening at 11am.

Major Theatres

Charles Playhouse
Home to *Sheer Madness*, America's longest-running non-musical play.
74 Warrenton St.
Tel: (617) 426 5225.

Colonial
106 Boylston St.
Tel: (617) 426 9366.

Emerson Majestic Theater
219 Tremont St.
Tel: (617) 824 8000.

Opera House
539 Washington St.
Tel: (617) 426 5300.

Schubert Theater
265 Tremont St.
Tel: (617) 426 4520 or (800) 447 7400.

Wang Center for the Performing Arts
270 Tremont St.
Tel: (617) 482 9393; www.wangcenter.org

Wilbur Theater
246 Tremont St.
Tel: (617) 931 2787.

American Repertory Theater
64 Brattle St, Cambridge.
Tel: (617) 547 8300; www.amrep.org

Huntington Theater
264 Huntington Ave.
Tel: (617) 266 0800;
www.huntingtontheater.com

The Lyric Stage
140 Clarendon St.
Tel: (617) 437 7172; www.lyricstage.com

Boston Center for the Arts
539 Tremont St.
Tel: (617) 426 5000.

Provincetown Theatre Company
74 Shankpainter Rd, Provincetown.
Tel: (508) 487 8673.
Provincetown Fringe Festival
1 Commercial St, Provincetown.
Tel: (508) 487 2666.

Dinner Theatres
Medieval Manor
246 East Berkeley St.
Tel: (617) 423 4900.
Mystery Café
290 Congress St.
Tel: (781) 320 0040.

Comedy Clubs
Catch a Rising Star
30 John F Kennedy St, Cambridge.
Tel: (617) 661 9887.
Comedy Connection
245 Quincy Market Place.
Tel: (617) 248 9700.
The Improv Asylum
216 Hanover St.
Tel: (617) 263 6887.
Also at:
247 Commercial St, Provincetown.
Tel: (508) 487 1430.
The Jungle
135 Bradford St. Provincetown.
Tel: (508) 487 9941.
Nick's Comedy Stop
100 Warrenton St.
Tel: (617) 482 0930.

Music Performance
Berklee College of Music
136 Massachusetts Ave.
Tel: (617) 395 9228.
Boston Ballet
Wang Center.
19 Clarendon St.
Tel: (617) 695 6950.
Fogg Art Museum
32 Quincy St.
Tel: (617) 495 9400.
Emmanuel Church
15 Newberry St.
Tel: (617) 536 3355.
Isabella Stewart Gardner Museum
280 The Fenway.
Tel: (617) 566 1401.
Kings Chapel
Tremont/School Sts.
Tel: (617) 523 1749.
New England Conservatory of Music
30 Gainsborough St.
Tel: (617) 585 1100;
www.newengland conservatory.edu
Boston Symphony Orchestra
301 Massachusetts Ave.
Tel: (617) 266 1200;
www.bso.org
Orpheum Theater
Hamilton Place, off Tremont St.
Tel: (617) 679 0810.

Dancing and Rock
Aria
246 Tremont St.
Tel: (617) 338 7080.

Axis
13 Landsdowne St.
Tel: (617) 262 2424.
Copperfield's
98 Brookline Ave.
Tel: (617) 247 8605.
Man-Ray
21 Brookline St, Cambridge.
Tel: (617) 864 0400;
www.manrayclub.com
Sugar Shack
1 Boylston Place.
Tel: (617) 351 2510.
Atlantic House
6 Masonic Pl, Provincetown.
Tel: (508) 487 3821.
Paramount
247 Commercial St, Provincetown.
Tel: (508) 487 1430.

Folk Music
Passim
47 Palmer St, Cambridge.
Tel: (617) 492 7679.

Jazz and Blues
Regattabar
Charles Hotel, 1 Bennett St, Cambridge.
Tel: (617) 661 5050.
Ryles
212 Hampshire St, Cambridge.
Tel: (617) 876 9330.
Scullers
400 Soldiers Field Rd.
Tel: (617) 562 4111.
Sophia's
1270 Boylston St.
Tel: (617) 351 7001.

Children

New England is the perfect place for youngsters to have fun and receive a painless education at the same time. The Greater Boston Visitors and Convention Bureau publishes *Kids Love Boston*, which is a children's guide to the area's major attractions.

Story Land

In Massachusetts both Plimoth Plantation and Old Sturbridge Village present historically accurate information in the most entertaining way possible. Both of these living history sites should be on every parent's itinerary.

In Boston, the **Children's Museum** (*see p31*) is a perennial favourite with children of all ages, with science, cultural activities and interactive learning fun. The **Museum of Science** (*see p41*) is also oriented towards the young, with plenty of hands-on exhibits on subjects as diverse as mathematics, optics and the human body. Even the driest subject is fun. The world's largest Van de Graaff generator, producing 15-ft bolts of lightning, pleases all ages, and younger children love to watch chicks hatch in the Giant Egg Incubator.

Franklin Park Zoo, which lies in part of the 'Emerald Necklace' (Boston's

Up in the air at Funtown USA, Old Orchard Beach, Maine, a hit for all ages

green belt), has a children's petting zoo, and in its African rainforest there are the sounds and sights of equatorial Africa, with 150 different animals from 50 species, including gorillas.
Franklin Park: Blue Hill Ave, Dorchester. Tel: (617) 451 5466. Open: Mon–Fri 10am–5pm, Sat–Sun 10am–6pm (winter 10am–4pm). Admission charge (half price first Sat of every month 10am–noon).

At the **New England Aquarium** (*see p42*) there are dolphin and sea lion shows in Discovery, a floating theatre. Street performers are always fun to watch: in good weather stop by at **Faneuil Hall Marketplace**, **Downtown Crossing** or **Harvard Square** in Cambridge for great, inexpensive entertainment. Before leaving Boston, a ride in the **Public Garden**'s swan boats is an absolute must.

Amusement Parks
One of New England's most child-friendly (and family budget-friendly) beach resorts is Old Orchard Beach in southern Maine, with two amusement parks offering different styles of entertainment. Palace Playland, by the pier, is right on the beach, and has a fireworks display on Thursday evenings. On Route 1 is the more elaborate Funtown/Splashtown. Both have all the favourite kiddie rides, including carousels and bumper cars, as well as thrill rides for older children.

Ben and Jerry's Ice Cream Factory
This is every child's dream destination – the home of Ben and Jerry's ice cream ('best in the world', according to *Time*).

Factory tours include free samples.
Route 100, Waterbury. Tel: (802) 244 5641. Open: daily 9am–6pm (9pm during Jul & Aug). Admission charge.

Story Land
North of Conway in New Hampshire's White Mountains, Story Land is a fantasy park that brings fairy tales to life. Kids can travel by pumpkin coach to Cinderella's castle, take an African safari, ride on an antique train, or even the Polar Coaster to the North Pole. There is also a petting farm with goats, sheep and pigs.
Route 16, Glen. Tel: (603) 383 4186. Open: Father's Day (mid-Jun)–Labor Day, daily 9am–6pm; Labor Day–Columbus Day (2nd Mon in Oct), weekends only 10am–5pm.

Clark's Trading Post
At the other end of the Kancamagus Highway is Clark's Trading Post in North Woodstock. This small theme park offers rides on the White Mountain Central Railroad; a standard-gauge wood-burning steam engine pulls the train over a covered bridge by the Pemigewasset River.
    Back at the trading post there is a family of native New Hampshire black bears, which perform throughout the day, a Mystical Mansion, a Rustic House that never fails to delight children with its bizarre surprises and the Mill Pond Bumper Boats, which help visitors to cool off on a hot day.
Route 3, North Woodstock. Tel: (603) 745 8913. Open: Jul–Aug, daily 10am–6pm; weekends only end-May–end-Jun & Sept–mid-Oct.

S p o r t   a n d   L e i s u r e

New Englanders are an understated bunch – except when it comes to sports. Loud and loyal fans of their sports teams, and active participants in a variety of outdoor activities, they love their sports. And there are a number of sports to love. New England has some of the nation's most admired professional sports teams, and a long tradition of college sports excellence. The huge quilt of forests, rivers, mountains and lakes that forms the New England landscape also boasts a bounty of recreational activities, which provide wonderful diversions for intrepid travellers.

American football is a major New England collegiate sport

SPECTATOR SPORTS

The Boston Marathon

Held every year since 1897, this is the world's oldest annual event and part of the Boston way of life. Every Patriot's Day (April) both spectators and participants gather for this impressive event.

Baseball

Few teams have a more illustrious history than the **Boston Red Sox**, New England's only major-league baseball team. The Red Sox won the first World Series ever played – in 1903 – and have had some of baseball's greatest play for them, including Babe Ruth, Ted Williams and Wade Boggs. After breaking 'The Curse', the team finally won the World Series again in 2004 and has become a favourite underdog-can-win team.

The baseball season begins early in April and ends in October. Teams from the American League bat it out on natural grass, playing about 80 home games a year.

The Red Sox play at Fenway Park, famous for the 'Green Monster' wall, in the heart of Kenmore Square. *Tel: (617) 267 9440, or (617) 482 4SOX for tickets; www.redsox.com*

New England is also home to a number of small leagues throughout the region; these provide the training for the next generation of major league stars. Check listings for minor league games in cities from Burlington to Pawtucket.

Basketball

The **Boston Celtics** are tied to the heart and soul of Boston. Named after the Bay City's substantial Irish population, the Celtics have won 16 National Basketball Association championships, more than any other professional team. The regular NBA season runs from October until April, with championship playoffs continuing until June.

The Celtics play at the TD Banknorth Garden.
Tel: (617) 624 1000; www.nba.com/celtics

American Football

The **New England Patriots** are now considered the team to be reckoned with after years of a bad reputation. Known for winning record numbers of consecutive games, the 'Pats' have become even more famous for their Superbowl victory streak beginning in 2001.

Twenty-eight National Football League teams take to the field (called the gridiron) every year. Pre-season action begins in early August. The regular season runs from early September to late December. Playoffs and the Super Bowl take the season into late January. The Patriots play at Gillette Stadium in Foxboro, about 45 minutes south of Boston. *Tel: (508) 543 1776; www.patriots.com*

The Patriots aren't the only team in town, however. Every autumn, loyal alumni from New England's many colleges head for university stadiums throughout the region.

Spend a balmy summer's evening watching a Red Sox game at Fenway Park baseball stadium

Here, tradition plays as much of a role as the game itself, as old friendships – and rivalries – are rekindled. Perhaps the most famous of these is the annual Harvard/Yale game, known simply as **The Game**. The competition, more than 100 years old, is the nation's longest-standing intercollegiate sporting event, pitting athletes from two of America's Ivy League universities against each other in a battle more over prestige and honour than athletic prowess.
For ticket information, call Harvard on tel: (617) 495 2211 or Yale on tel: (203) 432 1400. Check local listings for other college games.

Ice Hockey

Ice hockey, known simply as hockey in the US, migrated south from Canada a century ago and settled happily in the cold New England winter landscape. Today, it is among the most popular games in the region. Two professional teams and scores of collegiate teams constitute the core of spectator opportunities.

From November to April, the National Hockey League draws thousands to arenas to witness ice hockey being played at its best. The **Boston Bruins**, a founding team of the National Hockey League, play at the TD Banknorth Garden (*tel: (617) 624 1000; www.bostonbruins*). The **Hartford Wolfpack** (*tel: (820) 246 7825*) takes to the ice at the Hartford Civic Center in Hartford, Connecticut.

Some of America's finest collegiate hockey is also played on arenas throughout New England.

OTHER SPORTS

A number of other spectator sports rank among New Englanders' favourites, from horse racing to *jai alai* (pronounced 'high-a-lie') – an unusual court game resembling handball, in which players with long, curved wicker baskets catch and throw a hard ball against a wall. Local chambers of commerce or visitor bureaux can give you the specifics.

New Englanders enjoy the outdoors, and the region is full of summer and winter activities, from sailing along the Cape Cod coast to skiing down Stowe Mountain's well-groomed slopes. Following is a sampling of summer and winter sports.

Swimming

On a hot summer day, nothing could be finer than lounging along a Cape Cod beach, plunging into the icy waters off the Maine coast, or taking a dip in Vermont's Lake Champlain. Most of New England's best beaches are open to the public, so pack a picnic, bring plenty of sun screen – and get there early before the crowds. Note that, to locals, a 'beach' could refer to an area of imported sand on the edge of a lake where everyone swims.

Sailing

If you arrived by yacht, or you just love to sail, New England's wrinkled coast-line provides an ocean of opportunity for enjoying the open waters. Charters are available, and most harbours have a marina or dock to pull into for the night. For sailing without the salt, take advantage of the region's bounty of inland waters.

Snow tubing has become a popular winter activity

Surfing and Fishing

Surfers ride the waves off the coasts of Maine, Nantucket and Martha's Vineyard, while a growing legion of windsurfers can be found just about anywhere there is water.

New England also enjoys excellent fishing, whether in freshwater streams and lakes or surf-casting and deep-sea fishing. Wherever there is a harbour, someone will likely be offering fishing charters. Consult the local tourist bureau for specifics.

Golf and Tennis

New England is packed with champion-ship golf courses and excellent tennis facilities. The Professional Golf Association hosts tournaments at Pleasant Valley near Worcester, Massachusetts, and at a designated course in Hartford, Connecticut. The

Country Club at Brookline near Boston recently hosted the US Open golf championships. The *Yellow Pages* lists almost all public and private golf courses.

For racquet enthusiasts, the region has a rich history of tennis excellence, dating back to the inception of the US Pro Championships. The annual event, held at the Longwood Cricket Club near Boston, is one of professional tennis's longest-standing tournaments. The **Tennis Hall of Fame** in Newport, Rhode Island, hosts America's only grass-court tournament, just after Wimbledon. Visitors can find courts at many of New England's resorts and hotels; most city parks also have several courts available. For more information, contact the New England Tennis Association (*tel: (617) 964 2030*).

Skiing

New England is a snow sports lover's paradise. With abundant natural snow, and ski areas featuring the latest snow-making equipment, skiers will find near-perfect conditions most of the winter. Most areas offer savings on multi-day passes and lodging-ski packages.

Close to Boston, New Hampshire has 19 ski resorts with runs for all experience levels. In southern NH are Crotched Mountain and Pat's Peak, mid-state are Sunapee, Ragged Mountain, Tenney and Gunstock. In the northern tier are Waterville Valley, Attitash, Bretton Woods (the state's largest), Cranmore and Balsam's Wilderness. *www.skinh.com*

In Vermont, Killington's runs cover seven mountains, but Stowe and Stratton are also popular with New

Yorkers. Smuggler's Notch is one of the nation's most family-friendly large resorts, and Okemo, Bromley, Burke Mountain and Jay Peak are also known for their attention to family skiers. *www.skivermont.com*

Skiers head to Maine for Sugarloaf and Sunday River, two of the best-known areas, along with Saddleback, Black Mountain, Lost Mountain and Shawnee Peak. Most skiing is in the west central part of the state. *www.skimaine.com*

In Massachusetts there are small mountains in the central and western part of the state. While they do not have the altitude of more northern areas, they have enjoyable and challenging terrain. *http://skicentral.com/massachusetts.html*

Almost all of these resorts have cross-country (Nordic) and snow-shoeing facilities, and some of the finest experiences are at separate purpose-built facilities, in the northern states.

If you are thinking of a back-country trip, contact the **Appalachian Mountain Club** (*tel: (603) 466 2727*). It maintains several huts that stay open in winter for skiers and snowshoers.
For details of cycling, hiking, canoeing and kayaking, see pp146–7.

More on Skiing
Vermont Ski Areas Association *26 State St, Montpelier, Vermont 05602.*
Tel: (800) 223 2439 (toll free).
Appalachian Mountain Club *Box 298, Pinkham Notch, NH 03581.*
Tel: (603) 466 2727, or *AMC, 5 Joy St, Boston, Massachusetts 02108.*
Massachusetts Ski Hotline
Tel: (800) 227 MASS.
Ski NH at *www.skinh.com*

Food and Drink

New England has a reputation for good, honest, traditional food. Seafood is particularly good, with dishes like New England clam chowder (a thick, milk-based soup), fish cakes and fresh boiled lobster. Other regional specialities are Boston baked beans, Indian pudding and fried clams. 'Raw bars' serve fresh raw shellfish such as oysters. Clambakes are a New England tradition that should not be missed if the opportunity arises.

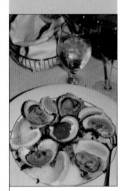

Oysters, a New England delicacy

What to Eat

Not all New England restaurants are good, of course. Some rely more on quantity than quality, and serve greasy, unimaginative food. Some American eating habits may seem curious to visitors. Biscuits are like unsweetened scones, and they are usually served smothered in thick white gravy – very often for breakfast! Fruit is an accompaniment to any meal, so don't be too surprised if your bacon and eggs come with a fruit salad on the same plate.

Vegetarians are generally well-served, particularly in cities. The Boston Vegetarian Society even holds a Food Festival every year in October.

Fast Food

McDonald's, KFC (Kentucky Fried Chicken) and Pizza Hut dominate New England, as they do the world. Wendy's and Burger King provide similar products at more or less the same price.

Coffee Shops

The coffee shop chains are one step above the fast-food operations and include Friendly's, Howard Johnson's (Ho Jo's) and Bickford's. They are often open 24 hours a day and serve decent food. They all have inexpensive children's menus, and you need never feel embarrassed at having boisterous children at your table.

Diners

The diner is a very American institution. Diners are not very different from coffee shops, generally smaller with a long counter to sit at. The traditional diner was designed to look like a railroad dining car with lots of chrome and a juke box. They served good, basic, cheap food without any frills. There are still a few around, but be careful; some diners have been 'yuppiefied', and they will not necessarily be the good, cheap eats you expect.

Breakfast

Diners and coffee shops (not the chains) are the best places for breakfast, and it is often served 24 hours a day. Eggs are the mainstay, and are often served with hash-brown potatoes, a choice of sausage, ham or bacon, and white or wholewheat bread or an English muffin. At weekends breakfast is eclipsed by brunch at the better restaurants. Usually served between 10am and 2pm, this leisurely meal is an elaborate, substantial breakfast-cum-lunch, sometimes accompanied by champagne.

Coffee is the main beverage, and it varies dramatically in quality from brown water to something a spoon will stand up in. As a rule of thumb, the cheaper the restaurant, the weaker the coffee. Refills are usually free for as long as you sit. Tea is less popular, and it is easy to see why. A cup of tea consists of a tea bag in tepid water, except in better restaurants.

Local Food

Fresh produce is always close at hand, and the Atlantic provides some of the finest fish and shellfish available. Over 23 million pounds of lobster are caught in Maine every year, in addition to excellent clams, mussels and scallops. The fish includes cod, for which Massachusetts is famous, haddock, sole, flounder and bass.

New England has neither the soil nor the climate to be a major agricultural producer, but it excels at speciality farming. Organic vegetables, heirloom varieties of tomatoes or potatoes, baby greens, fresh berries and other local crops are highly prized by better restaurants. It is not unusual to find menus describing a dish in detail, giving the local source of their farm products. The coastal bogs of Massachusetts provide the world's biggest supply of cranberries, without which every American's Thanksgiving dinner would be incomplete. These tart red berries are used for their juice and to make a sauce or jelly to accompany roast turkey. New England apples are exceptionally good, and there is a big cider industry. (American cider is really freshly pressed apple juice, but hard cider and applejack are alcoholic.)

Wherever you decide to eat in New England, you will almost certainly eat well – and for much less than you would pay for the equivalent meal at home.

Clambakes
A traditional clambake includes steaming lobsters, clams, corn-on-the-cob and potatoes in a deep hole in the shore, in which the wood fire has been allowed to burn to coals. Served in a restaurant, a clambake, while it may have all the ingredients, will not have been cooked in the traditional way.

Lobster clambake at Newport's Hyatt Regency Hotel

Where to Eat

The symbols below indicate restaurant price. The price ranges indicate the cost of a 2-course meal with wine.

★   under $15
★★ $15–$25
★★★ $25–$50
★★★★ over $50

BOSTON AREA

Aujourd'hui ★★★★
A spectacular view over the Public Garden, combined with above-average nouvelle cuisine.
Four Seasons Hotel, 200 Boylston St.
Tel: (617) 351 2071.

Bangkok Cuisine ★★
Great Thai food, near Symphony Hall.
177A Massachusetts Ave.
Tel: (617) 262 5377.

Bertucci's Brick Oven Pizzeria ★
Popular, above-average pizza place.
Look for the sign at locations throughout Boston.

Biba ★★★★
Eclectic cuisine in stylish surroundings.
272 Boylston St.
Tel: (617) 426 7878.

Boco Grande ★
Good, fresh self-service Mexican food.
149 1st St, Cambridge.
Tel: (617) 354 5550.

Caffe Vittoria ★
Italian café in Little Italy, with lots of atmosphere.
296 Hanover St.
Tel: (617) 227 7606.

Chez Henri ★★/★★★
French and Cuban fusion. Reservations suggested.
Shepherd St.
Tel: (617) 354 8980.

Chez Nous ★★★★
Excellent nouvelle cuisine in intimate atmosphere.
147 Huron Ave, Cambridge.
Tel: (617) 864 6670.

Daily Catch ★★
Great squid and fresh fish.
Several locations throughout Boston.

Dalí ★★/★★★
A good Spanish restaurant.
415 Washington St, Somerville.
Tel: (617) 661 3254.

Davide ★★★
Excellent Northern Italian cuisine.
326 Commercial Ave.
Tel: (617) 227 5745.

The Elephant Walk ★★/★★★
Upmarket Cambodian cuisine.
900 Beacon St.
Tel: (617) 247 1500.

Fire & Ice ★★
All-you-can-eat grill buffet, cooked to order while you watch.
50 Church St.
Tel: (617) 547 9007;
www.fire-ice.com

Giacomo's ★★
Great seafood.
355 Hanover St.
Tel: (617) 523 9026.

Hammersley's Bistro ★★★/★★★★
One of the great Boston restaurants, serving French-influenced dishes.
533 Tremont St.
Tel: (617) 423 2700.

Harvest ★★/★★★
Fine, varied cuisine with a garden courtyard.
44 Brattle St.
Tel: (617) 868 2255.

Legal Seafoods ★★★
Universally claimed to serve the best seafood in town. All the locations are always crowded.
Locations throughout Boston.

Locke-Ober Café ★★★★
A classic Boston restaurant turned to cutting-edge cuisine by a renowned chef.
3 Winter Place.
Tel: (617) 542 1340.

Mama Maria ★★★
Upmarket and intimate, with valet parking. Reservations suggested.
3 North Square.
Tel: (617) 523 0077.

Milk Street Café ★
Financial District café open for breakfast and lunch, serving good, inexpensive food including kosher meals.
50 Milk St.
Tel: (617) 542 3663.

Parker's ★★★
Great for brunch.
Omni Parker House,
60 School St.
Tel: (617) 227 8600.

Petit Robert Bistro ★★
French regional cuisine meets New England ingredients, with stunning results – and at very reasonable prices.
468 Commonwealth Ave.
Tel: (617) 375 0699.

Pho Pasteur ★
Theatre District authentic Vietnamese restaurant.
8 Kneeland St.
Tel: (617) 451 0247.

Ritz Dining Room ★★★★
Outstanding service, surroundings and food make this one of Boston's most memorable dining experiences.
Ritz Carlton Hotel,
15 Arlington St.
Tel: (617) 536 5700.

The Oak Room ★★★
Fine New England cuisine in Old Boston atmosphere.
Copley Plaza Hotel,
138 St James Ave.
Tel: (617) 267 5300.

Union Oyster House ★★
A landmark Boston restaurant and America's oldest.
41 Union St.
Tel: (617) 227 2750.

OUTSIDE BOSTON

Al Forno ★★★
Superb Northern Italian food, but no reservations can mean long waits.
577 South Main St,
Providence.
Tel: (401) 273 9760.

Bandol ★★★
People travel from Boston just to eat at this bright new star in Portland.
90 Exchange St,
Portland, Maine.
Tel: (207) 347 7155.

Blue Ginger ★★★/★★★★
Spectacular Asian fusion cuisine, chef Ming Tsai.
583 Washington St,
Wellesley.
Tel: (781) 283 5790.

Lucky Catch Cruises ★
Haul traps on a genuine working lobster boat, then take your catch next door to The Portland Lobster Co. where they will cook it and provide the accompaniments.
170 Commercial St,
Portland, Maine.
Tel: (207) 761 0941.
www.luckycatch.com

Salvation Café
Innovative and casual,

excellent fusion cuisine.
140 Broadway,
Newport, RI.
Tel: (401) 847 2620.

The Shaker Table ★★/★★★
The chef creates sumptuous feasts using only ingredients grown within a few miles of the village.
Canterbury Shaker Village,
Canterbury, New Hampshire.
Tel: (603) 783 4238.
www.shakers.org

Snowvillage Inn ★★
Elegant and creative dishes served in a warm country inn, on a hilltop with views of the White Mountains.
Snowville, New Hampshire. Tel: (603) 477 2818; (800) 447 4345.
www.snowvillageinn.com

White Horse Tavern ★★★★
Traditional New England food and atmosphere.
26 Marlborough St,
Newport.
Tel: (401) 849 3600.

There is no shortage of stylish restaurants

Maple Syrup

As the sap rises every spring, while snow is still on the ground, hundreds of sugarhouses throughout northern New England fire up their boilers to produce the sweet amber syrup of the sugar maple (as well as sugar and sweets or candy). This annual ritual was begun by the Native Americans.

Vermont alone accounts for over half a million gallons a year, more than any other state in the nation. Each mature tree produces about 10 gallons of sap, and it takes 30 to 40 gallons to produce one gallon of syrup. The rest is lost to evaporation.

Traditionally, the sap was collected in individual buckets attached to each tree, but now plastic tubing connects several trees to a collecting tank, or even directly to the sugarhouse.

For the 'sugaring-off' process, the sap is boiled in large, flat evaporating pans over wood or gas fires for up to 24 hours until it thickens. The syrup is filtered and graded according to colour. The choicest maple syrup is the lightest in colour.

Most sugarhouses welcome visitors. Look out for 'Maple Sugar' signs on the country roads, or ask at the local general store. Better still, you will also find them listed in *Maple Sugarhouses*, published by the Vermont Department of Agriculture (*116 State St, Montpelier, VT 05602; tel: (802) 828 2416*). Listings are by town, and give all details of the size of the sugarhouses, methods of operation and times of tours.

The season begins whenever there are freezing nights and a daytime temperature of 5–10°C/40–50°F to make the sap run. In southern Vermont this is usually at the end of February, through to late March or early April in the north. The season usually lasts three to four weeks.

You can still experience the process out of season at one of the museums devoted to the subject. The New England Maple Museum, Route 7, Pittsford, Vermont (*tel: (802) 483 9414*) is full of artefacts, and includes a free syrup tasting. The Maple Grove Maple Museum is the northern equivalent, off Highway I-91 in St Johnsbury.

Facing page: the Northern Countryside is full of signs that tempt you to buy maple syrup;
below: the smell of springtime, making maple syrup in Vermont

Hotels and Accommodation

New England has an enormous variety of accommodation, and most of it is relatively inexpensive compared with the rest of the world. It is also of an almost universally high standard. Even the cheapest places are clean and well appointed. However, this is not the case with inner-city residential hotels, which cater to transients, and often look as though they went out of business decades ago.

Fifteen Beacon Hotel, Boston

Motels

The motel, of course, is the uniquely American lodging. For the budget-conscious traveller, these are by far the best places to stay. The chain motels are perhaps the most predictable for quality, but there are fewer in New England than in other areas of America, so it pays to book ahead. They all provide a clean, simply decorated room, usually with the choice of twin or double beds. There is always a television, a telephone in all but the most basic, and always a bathroom or shower and toilet adjoining the room.

Payment is usually in advance, rooms will be held only until 5pm unless the reservation is secured with a credit card.

Motels tend to be on the outskirts of cities on the main roads, and are rarely convenient for sightseeing. If you have a car, this should not present a problem. Motels are usually very well advertised with roadside signs. Most cities have a motel strip (Boston is a notable exception). The closest motel area to Boston is north on Route 1, well outside the city limits. If in doubt, any local should be able to tell you where to go.

Breakfast is rarely included at motels. There is usually a restaurant close by, and vending machines for soft drinks. Complimentary coffee is sometimes provided in the lobby (reception).

Good, very inexpensive chains are:
Motel 6 (*tel: (800) 437 7486*);
Days Inn (*tel: (800) 325 2525*);
Super 8 (*tel: (800) 800 8000*).
Also very good but not as cheap are:
Travelodge (*tel: (800) 255 3050*);
Comfort Inn (*tel: (800) 221 2222*);
Best Western (*tel: (800) 528 1234*);
Howard Johnson's (*tel: (800) 654 2000*).

Bed and Breakfast Inns

Unlike in the UK, in New England bed and breakfast (B&B) inns often means an elegantly restored Victorian- or Colonial-era home with private baths and a multi-course breakfast. The best way to distinguish these from their homey counterparts is by the price. Not all B&Bs are in country villages. City B&Bs such as The Gryphon House, which occupies a stylish Back Bay town house in Boston (*www.innboston.com*), offer personal hospitality at reasonable prices. It is often hard to draw a line between smaller inns and the more stylish bed & breakfast lodges.

Hotels

Full-service hotels are much more expensive than motels, and they are generally only found in the cities.

There are some excellent hotels in New England for those who can afford them, a few of which could be described as classic. For the ultimate in both luxury and service, these are undeniably the places to stay.

Some luxury hotels are quite historic, classic bastions of elegance and fine service with modernised facilities. Others are thoroughly modern, built in the standard module of new hotels.

Classics

Boston – **Fairmont Copley Plaza**; **The Lenox, The Ritz-Carlton**; Providence, RI – **The Biltmore**; Hanover, NH – **The Hanover Inn**; Deerfield, MA – **The Deerfield Inn**; Hartford, CT – **The JP Morgan Hotel**.

Modern

Boston – **The Four Seasons, The Boston Harbor Hotel**; Cambridge – **The Charles Hotel**; Providence, RI – **The Westin**; Newport, RI – **Vanderbilt's**.

Even in hotels of this quality, breakfast is rarely included in the price, although there is a growing trend to include a continental breakfast at some hotels.

Gryphon House Inn, Boston

Mountain View Grand Hotel and Resort, Whitefield NH

Resort Hotels

Also at the top end of the market are resort hotels, which not only provide de luxe service and surroundings, but also a range of sports, including tennis and golf, and often spa facilities. Once you have checked into one of these luxury resorts, there is no need to set foot in the outside world again until your money runs out. Some of the best resort hotels are:

Cape Cod – **Chatham Bars Inn**;
Manchester, VT – **The Equinox**;
White Mountains, NH – **The Balsams**, **The Mount Washington Hotel** and **The Wentworth**;
Connecticut – **The Norwich Inn**.

Hotel Chains

Most of the big international hotel chains have properties in Boston and New England. They provide options at reasonable prices but without the glamour of a landmark building. They are usually conveniently located near the main tourist attractions:

Doubletree (*tel: (800) 528 0444*);
Hilton (*tel: (800) 445 8667*);
Holiday Inn (*tel: (800) 465 4329*);
Hyatt (*tel: (800) 228 900*);
Marriott (*tel: (800) 228 9290*);
Ramada (*tel: (800) 272 6232*);
Sheraton (*tel: (800) 325 3535*).

Reservations

It is always wise to make reservations, particularly during the peak season and special events. In making reservations for any accommodation make sure it is in a convenient location. Ask plenty of questions. It is also worth asking if there are any special rates available. Many places will give significant discounts rather than lose the business; it never does any harm to ask.

Several chains offer discounts if vouchers are purchased outside of the US. These include:
Howard Johnson's – Freedom North America;
Vagabond – Discover America Hotel Pass;
Tourcheck America handles bookings for Best Western, Hilton, Holiday Inn, Ramada, Travelodge and Quality Inn hotels and motels.

Most travel agents should be aware of these programmes and have vouchers available for purchase.

Long-distance calls from in-room telephones can be outrageously expensive, and there is often a charge even for reverse-charge or credit-card calls. Always find out what these charges are to avoid a nervous shock when it is too late. All hotels and motels have public telephones available in the lobby areas. Many hotels do not charge for local calls, but paradoxically it is usually the cheaper places that have this policy. Again, check before use.

In-room mini-bars are another big profit-maker for hotels. Liquor is so cheap in most New England states that if you enjoy a nightcap, it is cheaper to buy a full bottle at a liquor store than to buy a miniature from a mini-bar.

The Mount Washington Hotel and Resort, Bretton Woods

On Business

Business practices in the United States are the same as in Europe. International business in the English-speaking world has become so uniform it can be difficult to know which country you are in.

Customs House, Salem

The general visa and immigration rules (*see p174*) apply to business travellers intending to leave the country within a six-month period. Special visas are necessary for extended stays and for permission to work in the United States. The availability of these is dependent upon circumstances, and accurate advice should be sought from the closest American Consulate.

Boston is the only major international business centre in New England. The main industries are computers, finance, trade, high-tech, publishing and education. Other important industries include: printing, shipbuilding, sugar-refining, boot and shoe manufacture, electrical machinery, textiles, bakery products and confectionery, cutlery, leather, plastics, chemicals, furniture, foundry and machine-shop products and meat packing.

Hartford, Connecticut, is the world centre for the insurance industry. It is also the home of United Technologies. Other significant industries include manufacturing, finance, precision tools, brushes, revolvers, dishwashers, glass-making machines, power transmission chains, airplane engines and propellers, counting devices, electrical equipment and auto parts. Hartford is also a tobacco-growing centre.

Banks
Major European banks are represented in Boston. Few banks have foreign exchange facilities, but any bank can receive payments wired from overseas. It is preferable to have the money wired in US dollars to avoid unnecessary delays and often high bank charges. Banking hours are generally from 9am to 5pm, but this varies from bank to bank.

Business Hours
Most offices are open Monday to Friday from 9am to 5pm. Many in-town business support services, including office supply shops, close over the weekend, but those located in suburban shopping malls stay open all week. Post offices open briefly on Saturday mornings in most towns.

Business Media
Boston (newspapers/magazines)
Adweek/New England, Banker and Tradesman, Boston Business Journal, Boston Globe, Boston Herald, Harvard Business Review, Industry, New England Business, New England Economic Review.
(TV/radio)
CNN – cable television channel giving regular business and stock market news throughout the day.
WBZ-AM 1030 – ABC affiliate radio

programme with occasional business coverage.

WHDH-AM 850 – NBC affiliate.
WUMB-FM 91.9 – public broadcasting station which carries BBC World Service news.

Hartford
The Business Journal, Business Times, The Hartford Courant.

Conference/Exhibition Sites
Boston
Bayside Expo Center, *Dorchester Vernon St. Tel: (617) 474 6000; fax: (617) 265 8434.*
Boston Park Plaza Hotel and Towers, *64 Arlington St. Tel: (617) 426 2000. www.bostonparkplaza.com*
Hynes Convention Center, *900 Boylston St. Tel: (617) 954 2000; fax: (617) 954 2125.*
Marriott Hotel, *Copley Place, 110 Huntington Ave. Tel: (617) 236 5800. www.marriott.com*
Northeast Trade Center and Exhibition Hall, *100 Sylvan Rd, Woburn. Tel: (617) 935 8090.*
World Trade Center, *164 Northern Ave. Tel: (617) 385 5000; fax: (617) 439 5090.*
Westford Regency Inn and Conference Center, *219 Littleton Rd, Westford, MA 01886. Tel: (508) 692 8200.*

Hartford, Connecticut
Hartford Civic Center, *1 Civic Center Plaza. Tel: (212) 465 6741. www.hartfordciviccenter.com*

Providence, Rhode Island
Dunkin' Donuts Center, *1 LaSalle Sq. Tel: (401) 331 0700.*

International Courier Services
DHL Worldwide Express, *Tel: (1 800) 225 5345. www.dhl.com*
Federal Express, *Tel: (1 800) GO-FEDEX. www.fedex.com*
United States Postal Service, *Tel: (1 800) 725 2161. www.usps.com*

Secretarial Services
Most hotels have at least basic executive services and facilities. Several provide full secretarial services and a growing number have in-room modems. Secretarial facilities are listed in the *Yellow Pages*. The HQ Headquarters Companies, *124 Mt Auburn Street, Cambridge* (*tel: (617) 547 0222*) offer a full range of services.

Translation Services
AT & T Language Line Services
Tel: (1 800) 752 6096, ext 409 – toll free.
Harvard Translations
Tel: (617) 868 6800.

Transportation
Aircraft charter companies providing helicopters, Lear jets and smaller fixed-wing aircraft:
Boston
Executive Fliteways
Tel: (1 800) 533 3363.
Flight Time International
Tel: (781) 891 0405.
Wiggins Airways *Tel: (800) 877 5690.*
Delta Jet *Tel: (617) 776 6670.*

Hartford
Executive Aviation
Tel: (800) 393 2884.
Million Air *Tel: (203) 548 9334.*

Practical Guide

Arriving

Entry Requirements

Citizens of Australia, New Zealand, Ireland and the UK (as well as citizens of most western European countries and Japan) need only a valid machine-readable passport to enter the USA if their stay is less than 90 days, they have a return ticket and have arrived on an airline participating in the visa-waiver programme (most major carriers). Canadian citizens need only identification and proof of residence. Citizens of South Africa and most other countries must present a passport and tourist visa.

Travellers who require visas should obtain them from a US consulate or embassy in their country of residence, as they are difficult to obtain elsewhere. In the UK your Thomas Cook travel consultant can advise.

While in the US, visitors can take a side trip overland or by sea into Canada or Mexico and re-enter without a visa, within their overall 90-day stay.

Immigration laws are both complicated and strictly enforced, and it is advisable to check with the American Consulate well before departure.

By Air

Logan International Airport is the main airport for international flights into New England, handling over 60 airlines. Virtually all international visitors will come through Logan.

Bradley International Airport in Connecticut and Bangor International Airport in Maine handle some international traffic, but they are mainly used for domestic routings. Sometimes it can be less expensive to fly into New York's Kennedy Airport and get a connecting flight to one of the New England airports.

Domestic flights are generally very expensive, with the exception of the services between Boston and New York. If planning short hops within New England or flying in from another state, it is advisable to purchase a ticket before arrival. Airport taxes are included in the price of the ticket. Several airlines offer Visit USA passes, and travel agents should be able to advise on the best deals.

Logan International Airport has five terminals. Terminals B, C and E serve international scheduled flights. A free bus service links them, with a separate free service for travellers with disabilities. Terminals C and E have foreign exchange facilities and information booths, although neither is 24-hour.

There are duty-free shops in Departures. All terminals cater for travellers with disabilities, with lifts, ramps, adapted toilets and amplified phones. Terminal C has a 24-hour nursery, and all terminals have catering facilities.

The airport stands on a peninsula facing the city. It therefore takes only seven minutes to reach the city centre by the water shuttle (take the free bus from the terminal to the shuttle departure point), but 30 minutes by taxi and 20 to 30 minutes by the MBTA, called the T. Silver Line buses connect all terminals to

Boston's T service is efficient, clean and user-friendly; its four lines intersect downtown

South Station, on the Red Line. The T is by far the cheapest option. There are many express bus services from the airport to outlying areas of Boston (*for information, call freephone: 1 800 23 LOGAN*).

By Rail
Amtrak rail services connect Boston South and Boston Back Bay stations with Providence, New Haven and New York City, and New Haven and other New England towns with Montreal. Amtrak timetables are published in the *Thomas Cook Overseas Timetable* (*see p185*).

Camping
New England in the summer is ideal for camping holidays, and outside the major cities there is no shortage of campsites. State parks and national forests have excellent camping facilities, but reservations must be made in some if you are planning a visit during the peak season. Information can be obtained from the state tourism offices. Camper vans – called motor homes or RVs (recreational vehicles) in the US – are available for hire from specialist companies. One of the largest is **Cruise America** (*tel: (800) 327 7778*). Smaller

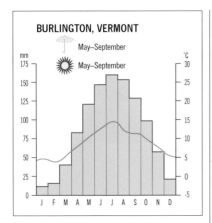

BURLINGTON, VERMONT

May–September

May–September

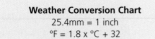

Weather Conversion Chart
25.4mm = 1 inch
°F = 1.8 x °C + 32

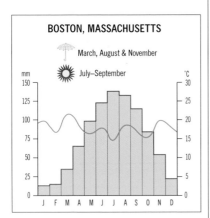

BOSTON, MASSACHUSETTS

March, August & November

July–September

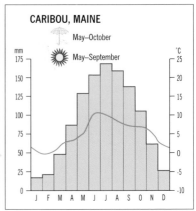

CARIBOU, MAINE

May–October

May–September

older children sharing their parents' room. Larger hotels offer safe and reliable babysitting services. Many restaurants have children's menus. Highchairs are universally available. Children are not allowed in bars unless meals are served.

Diapers (nappies) and food for infants are available at any supermarket or drugstore, and in most towns can be found 24 hours a day in at least one convenience store. Baby milk, called infant formula, is available in several dairy and non-dairy varieties. Prices are very reasonable.

New England is generally very safe for tourists, but never leave children unattended. Take care on the coast – the Atlantic Ocean can be very dangerous even on the most beautiful day. Take heed of all warning signs.

Climate

The best months for travelling in New England are generally from mid-May to mid-October. Many attractions outside the cities are only open during this period. New England has very distinct

local companies are listed in the *Yellow Pages* under Motor Homes – Renting and Leasing. It may be cheaper to pre-book through your own travel agent.

Children

Many hotels provide cribs (cots) for free, and extra beds at a nominal charge for

seasons. The winter is very cold, with frequent snowfalls, but often blue skies. Spring is the season of maple syrup, with cold nights and fresh days. Summer is generally pleasantly warm but can be hot and humid. Autumn can be the best season of all, with sunny, crisp days and spectacular foliage. Maine, Vermont and New Hampshire have five seasons: the usual, plus the Mud Season in April, after the snow and before the flowers!

Consulates General

Australia *20 Beacon St, Boston.* *Tel: (617) 542 8655.*
Canada *3 Copley Place, Boston.* *Tel: (617) 262 3760.*
Ireland *535 Boylston St, Boston.* *Tel: (617) 267 9330.*
UK *600 Atlantic Ave, Boston.* *Tel: (617) 248 9555.*

Crime

Crime is a very real problem but should be put into perspective, and is no worse than other major cities of the world. Be street smart and alert to your surroundings, as you would be in any city. Stay out of seedy neighbourhoods and don't wander from well lighted and populated areas after dark. Try to avoid getting into a confrontational situation with anyone. Also, it is unwise to pick up hitchhikers. A more real problem is theft from cars left on the street in major cities. Take sensible precautions and make sure valuables are not on display. Carry traveller's cheques, rather than cash. All hotels and most shops and restaurants accept US dollar cheques. Both VISA and American Express are widely

Conversion Table

FROM	TO	MULTIPLY BY
Inches	Centimetres	2.54
Feet	Metres	0.3048
Yards	Metres	0.9144
Miles	Kilometres	1.6090
Acres	Hectares	0.4047
Gallons	Litres	4.5460
Ounces	Grams	28.35
Pounds	Grams	453.6
Pounds	Kilograms	0.4536
Tons	Tonnes	1.0160

To convert back, for example from centimetres to inches, divide by the number in the third column.

Men's Suits

UK	36	38	40	42	44	46	48
Rest of Europe	46	48	50	52	54	56	58
USA	36	38	40	42	44	46	48

Dress Sizes

UK		8	10	12	14	16	18
France		36	38	40	42	44	46
Italy		38	40	42	44	46	48
Rest of Europe		34	36	38	40	42	44
USA		6	8	10	12	14	16

Men's Shirts

UK	14	14.5	15	15.5	16	16.5	17
Rest of Europe	36	37	38	39/40	41	42	43
USA	14	14.5	15	15.5	16	16.5	17

Men's Shoes

UK	7	7.5	8.5	9.5	10.5	11
Rest of Europe	41	42	43	44	45	46
USA	8	8.5	9.5	10.5	11.5	12

Women's Shoes

UK	4.5	5	5.5	6	6.5	7
Rest of Europe	38	38	39	39	40	41
USA	6	6.5	7	7.5	8	8.5

recognised and provide fast service in the case of loss.

Customs Regulations

Everyone entering the US must pass through US Customs. Personal allowances for visitors include one US quart (0.9464 litre) of spirits or wine, 300 cigarettes or 50 cigars, plus up to $100-worth of gifts. In practice, most of these items are far cheaper in the US than at airport duty-free shops, so there is little point importing them.

There is no restriction on the amount of currency imported or exported, but anything over $10,000 must be declared.

US Customs are particularly concerned about drugs, animals, meat (both fresh and processed), plants and fresh fruit. Penalties are severe.

Driving

Drivers need a valid licence from their home country. International Driver's Permits are generally unnecessary. Road signs use international symbols.

Major roads are well surfaced and well signed. In some rural areas there are sections of unpaved road. Motorways are called highways or Interstates.

Rules of the Road

Traffic drives on the right. The speed limit on highways is 55mph unless otherwise posted. In town the limit is between 25 and 35mph. Speed limits are always well signposted and strictly enforced. On Interstates you can be ticketed for driving too slowly in the left-hand lane. The low speed limits mean that freeway driving is generally safe. In cities there is a continual problem with

The Maine Lobsterman, Portland

drivers anticipating traffic lights or trying to make it through on amber. Always be careful at these junctions, as there is usually no delay phase in the lights. Avoid drink-driving at all costs as it is strictly prohibited. Keep any alcohol unopened and in the boot.

Signs

There are many minor junctions where there is a stop sign in only one direction, and they are often not clearly marked. Pay particular attention when driving off the main roads. If you have to drive in Boston, plan your journey ahead of time. Highways can be so complicated that a missed turn-off can result in a lot of frustration.

Petrol (Gas)

New England is ideal for car touring, and there is no shortage of petrol stations and garage facilities. Petrol (called gas, short for gasoline) is sold in unleaded regular, intermediate and super. Diesel is also available at most gas stations.

Maps

All gas stations have good maps for sale, and most car rental companies have local maps free of charge. The main motoring organisation in the US is the American Automobile Association (called the Triple A). The AAA has reciprocal agreements with overseas motoring organisations, and both roadside assistance and free route maps are available upon presentation of your membership card.

Car Hire

It is usually better to arrange for a car before arriving. Several airlines have special deals available with preferential rates if the booking is made in advance. Try to make a reservation, as certain categories of car may be in short supply during peak holiday seasons.

Automatic transmission is usual in all rental cars. American cars are big, and a so-called mid-size is huge by European standards. The smallest size available is the sub-compact, which will just carry four people and a small amount of luggage. For summer travel, ask for a car with air conditioning, usually available at no extra cost.

None of the major car rental companies will rent to anyone under the age of 25. It may be possible to find a local company that will, but be prepared to pay a loaded insurance premium.

If you hire a car, collision insurance, often called collision damage waiver or CDW, is normally offered by the hirer, and is usually compulsory. Check with your own motor insurers before you leave, as you may be covered by your normal policy. If not, CDW is payable locally and may be as much as 50 per cent of the hiring fee. Neither CDW nor your personal travel insurance will protect you for liability arising out of an

Ferry, Portland harbour

accident in a hire car. You should obtain such extra cover, preferably from your travel agent or other insurer, or as part of the rental contract.

Breakdowns and Accidents
In case of breakdown, immediately inform the car rental company and await instructions. In case of accident:
1. Set up warning signs. Flares are usually used and are available from any auto store.
2. Call police and an ambulance if required. The emergency telephone number is 911.
3. Take the names and addresses of all involved, the make and licence plate number of the other vehicle, and the names and numbers of insurance policies.
4. Write down names and addresses of any witnesses, together with the time and date of the accident. If possible, take photographs of the accident from several angles.
5. Never, under any circumstances, admit to, or sign, any statement of responsibility.

Electricity
The standard supply is 110 volts at 60 cycles. Flat two-pin plugs are used universally.

Emergency Telephone Numbers
For police, fire and ambulance dial 911.
Thomas Cook traveller's cheque refund is a 24-hour service. Report loss or theft within 24 hours, *tel: (00 44) 1733 318950 (toll free)*.
MasterCard card replacement: *tel: (1 800) 622 7747 (toll free)*.

Health
There are no mandatory vaccination requirements. It is advisable to keep tetanus immunisation up to date. The standard of health care is extremely high, but so are the costs. It is essential to have a good insurance policy. Many doctors and hospitals refuse to give treatment without proof of insurance.
All major hospitals have 24-hour emergency rooms. Information on general and specialist medical aid can be obtained from hotels or listings in the *Yellow Pages*. New England does not have many specific health problems. Tap water is obviously safe, but if hiking in the back country, do not drink from the streams, as the water often carries the intestinal parasite giardia. A real problem is Lyme disease, contracted from ticks found in long grass.
AIDS is a continuing concern and, needless to say, suitable precautions are an absolute necessity.

Hitchhiking
Hitchhiking is only illegal on freeways. However, it is not recommended in New England. Motorists are very wary of hitchhikers, and it can be very difficult to get lifts.

Insurance
You should take out personal travel insurance before leaving, from your travel agent, tour operator or insurance company. It should give adequate cover for medical expenses, loss and theft and personal liability (but liability arising from motor accidents is not usually included; *see under* Car Hire, *p179*), and

also covers cancellation expenses. Always read the conditions, and check that the amount of cover is adequate. Remember that medical treatment can be very expensive in the US.

Laundry

All major hotels have one-day laundry and dry-cleaning services from Monday to Friday. Alternatively, there are many dry cleaners offering a two- to four-hour service; check the *Yellow Pages*.

Launderettes are also available.

Maps

General maps are available from car hire companies. More detailed town maps and walking maps are usually available free of charge at chambers of commerce and visitor bureaux, which are listed in the *Yellow Pages*.

Measurements

America still uses the imperial system of measurement. The only difference is that the US gallon, quart and pint are 20 per cent smaller than the UK versions.

Media

The closest there is to a national daily newspaper in New England is the *Boston Globe*. Boston is also the home of the *Christian Science Monitor*, which is considered by many to be one of the world's most unbiased publications. In most towns you can find both the *Wall*

Cruise ship passing the Portland Head Lighthouse

Street Journal and the *New York Times*, which often give a more global view.

For local news, keep the car radio tuned to one of the news stations.

In most parts of New England it is possible to receive a Public Broadcasting Service (PBS) station. Virtually every hotel and motel room has a television. More often than not, it will be cable TV, offering 30 channels or more. As with radio, there are usually two or three PBS stations; these give good news coverage, and most of the other programmes are British.

Money Matters

Banking hours are usually 10am–5pm Monday to Friday, some being open on Saturdays as well.

Traveller's cheques must be in US dollars. They are accepted in shops, hotels and restaurants. Most banks do not offer foreign exchange facilities, and most visitors exchange money at the airport or hotel. Thomas Cook MasterCard Traveller's Cheques free you from the hazards of having large amounts of cash, and in the event of loss or theft can quickly be refunded (*see* Emergency Telephone Numbers, *p180*).

If you need to transfer money quickly, you can use the MoneyGram℠ Money Transfer service. (*For more details in the UK, telephone Freephone 0800 897198.*)

All major credit cards are universally accepted in New England. Paper currency is available in denominations of 1, 5, 10, 20, 50 and 100 dollars. Although the bills look very similar, the

Maple syrup for sale

value is clearly printed in each corner on both sides. Coins come in pennies (1 cent), nickels (5 cents), dimes (10 cents), quarters (25 cents) and 50-cent pieces. Keep a few quarters handy for parking meters, telephones and newspapers.

Sales tax is added to the price of all goods and restaurant meals in New England, with the sole exception of New Hampshire, which has no sales tax, but does tax meals and lodging. Tax rates range from 4 to 7.5 per cent.

There are no restrictions on the amount of money that can be brought into or taken out of the US (*see* Customs Regulations, *p178, for more information*).

National Holidays
New Year's Day (1 January)
Martin Luther King Day
(3rd Monday in January)
Lincoln's Birthday (12 February)
Washington's Birthday
(3rd Monday in February)
Memorial Day (last Monday in May)
Independence Day (4 July)
Labor Day
(1st Monday in September)
Columbus Day
(2nd Monday in October)
Veterans Day (11 November)
Thanksgiving
(4th Thursday in November)
Christmas Day (25 December).

Patriots Day is celebrated in Massachusetts on the third Monday of April.

Government offices, including post offices, are closed for most of these holidays, but few places observe them all. Shops remain open on all holidays except Thanksgiving and Christmas.

Opening Hours
Shops in malls are open seven days a week, typically from 10am to 6pm, and from noon on Sundays. Smaller shops, those on downtown 'main streets', and more specialised businesses close on Sundays.

Most offices, including government offices, open Monday to Friday 9am–5pm.

For museums and art galleries, opening times vary dramatically.

Organised Tours
The majority of people visiting New England hire cars, undoubtedly the best way to see the region. However, in cities, bus tours save parking headaches and ensure that nothing major is missed. There are both ordinary and specialised bus tours available in Boston. If time is limited, an ordinary tour may fit the bill, but it will be fairly superficial. Dozens of tour operators serve New England:
Gray Line (*tel: (781) 986 6100*) offers three-hour Boston and Cambridge tours, good for orientation. For serious sightseeing, **Old Town Trolley** has one-hour tours with an all-day pass on the tour route, so that you can get off and visit sights at leisure on the way. They also offer special interest tours, such as a three-hour 'JFK's Boston' or the three-hour evening 'Gravestones' tour. **Boston History Collaborative** offers the literary sites of Boston and Concord, Boston inventions and maritime sites. City walking tours are offered by **National Park Service** rangers. Food lovers will

be especially interested in **North End Italian Market Tours**, led by an expert in Italian cuisine (*tel: (617) 523 6032; www.cucinare.com*).

Specialised Tours
Boston by Foot *Tel: (617) 367 2345.*
Concord Copters *Tel: (617) 247 3777.*
Old Town Trolley Tours *Tel: (617) 269 7010.*
Pitcairn Tours *Tel: (617) 696 8130.*

Pharmacies
Most pharmacies are open from at least 9am until 6pm. Drugstores, usually open till 9pm, have a pharmacy counter for dispensing prescriptions. Drugstores are like mini-supermarkets, with a wide range of products on sale.

Places of Worship
New England was founded on a strongly Protestant base, but today virtually every religion has a presence. Newspapers generally list times of services for the main denominations. A comprehensive list under 'Churches' in the *Yellow Pages* includes mosques and Buddhist temples; synagogues have their own listing.

Police
Every incorporated city and most towns have their own police force with normal police responsibilities, including traffic control. For any emergency in New England, call 911.

Post Offices
Post offices are generally open Monday to Friday 9am–5pm. They are always closed on Sundays. Stamps are available from vending machines in some hotels

and shops, but they cost more than from a post office. Postage rates change frequently, so always check on current tariffs. An airmail letter or postcard takes about one week to travel from New England to Europe. Surface mail has been known to take three months! Appropriate containers for parcels are sold at the post office. A Customs declaration form must accompany any parcel being mailed abroad.

Poste restante is known as 'general delivery'. To collect you need some form of identification. Letters can be addressed to any post office and must include the zip code. Mail is held for only 30 days, after which it is returned to the sender whose name and address should be on the envelope. Telegrams are sent from Western Union offices, not from post offices. If you have a credit card, you can dictate a telegram over the telephone and charge it. Western Union offices are listed in the *Yellow Pages*.

Public Transport
The majority of New Englanders drive cars and, outside of Boston, the state of Rhode Island, and some larger cities, the public transportation system is not well developed.

Local rail, metro (the T) and bus services in Boston are operated by MBTA over a very dense network. A main-line rail service connects Boston and Hyannis, and commuter rail lines connect Boston with Providence, Salem, Gloucester and other points.

A network of long-distance buses, run by various companies, serves the whole of New England and provides connections to New York State and

Canada. Full details and timetables can be found in the *Thomas Cook Overseas Timetable*, published bi-monthly and obtainable from branches of Thomas Cook, by telephoning the order line in the UK on *(01733) 416477* or buy online at *www.thomascookpublishing.com*

Greyhound is the major operator travelling between all the main cities. On some of the longer routes, Greyhound is not significantly cheaper than the cheapest air ticket. For the greatest saving, buy a Greyhound Discovery Pass, which is available for 4 to 60 days, and must be purchased outside the US. Buy online at *www.discoverypass.com*. Local offices in New England can be found in the *Yellow Pages*. Taxis are available in all towns of any size, but are expensive.

Senior Citizens

Most hotels, motels, restaurants and museums have preferential rates for senior citizens. Usually they want to see some form of identification, but often just looking old enough is sufficient – which can be very demoralising!

Smoking

Throughout the US, smoking has declined so dramatically that smokers are very much the exception rather than the rule, and are generally looked upon as social pariahs. Smoking is not allowed on public transport, in public buildings and in many workplaces. Hotels offer non-smoking rooms, and car hire companies offer smoke-free cars. Restaurants still have small smoking sections, but they are indeed small.

Boston from the Esplanade

View of Mount Washington

Telephones

Apart from telephone booths (kiosks), there are public telephones in most bars, restaurants, hotel lobbies and gas stations. All public telephones accept 5-, 10- and 25-cent coins, with 30 cents being the minimum charge. In airports there are often telephones that allow the call to be charged to a credit card.

Hotels usually charge a high premium for calls from the room. Conversely, some hotels allow local calls at no cost. Reverse-charge calls, 'collect calls', can be made from any telephone by calling the operator. Dial 0 for the local operator (00 for a long-distance operator).

All numbers with an 800 or 1 800 prefix are toll-free. At a public telephone insert a dime first, which will be returned when you hang up. For international calls dial 011, the country code, then the number. The cheapest time for transatlantic calls is between 11pm and 7am.

International codes are:
Australia *61*
Canada *no code from US*

Ireland *353*
New Zealand *64*
UK *44*

Local directory information: *411*
Long-distance directory enquiries: dial relevant area code, then *555 1212*
Toll-free enquiries: *(800) 555 1212.*

Thomas Cook

Thomas Cook's website, at *www.thomascook.com*, provides up-to-the-minute details of Thomas Cook's travel and foreign money services.

Time

New England is on Eastern Standard Time, five hours behind GMT. Daylight saving time, when clocks go forward by one hour, operates from the last Sunday in April to the first Sunday in October.

Tipping

Tips are a way of life, and everyone in the service industry in the United States expects them. They are very rarely included in the bill, except sometimes in restaurants. You should always check. The amount is, of course, always at the discretion of the customer.

Toilets

Public toilets, or restrooms, are usually clean and free, with soap and paper, but not always easy to find. In cities they can be found in department stores, bars, restaurants and all gas stations.

Beacon Hill's varied architecture

Tourist Offices

For maps, comprehensive brochures and referrals to local chambers of commerce for more specific information, the following addresses are useful:

Connecticut Tourism Division

Department of Economic Development, 865 Brook St, Rocky Hill, CT 06067. Tel: (800) 282 6863. www.ctbound.org

Maine Office of Tourism

#59 State House Station, Augusta, ME 04333. Tel: (207) 623 0363, (888) MAINE45. www.visitmaine.com

Massachusetts Office of Travel and Tourism

10 Park Plaza, Suite 4510, Boston, MA 02116. Tel: (617) 973 8500. www.massvacation.com

New Hampshire Office of Travel and Tourism

Box 1856, Concord, NH 03302. Tel: (603) 271 2665. www.visitnh.gov

Rhode Island Tourism Division

1 West Exchange St, Providence, RI 02903. Tel: (401) 222 2601, (800) 556 2484. www.visitrhodeisland.com

Vermont Travel Department

134 State St, Montpelier, VT 05602. Tel: (802) 828 3236, (800) VERMONT. www.1-800-vermont.com

Travellers with Disabilities

The US is more alert to the needs of visitors with disabilities than many countries. Airports always have good facilities, including special lifts, toilets and wheelchairs. Most hotels, public buildings and museums have wheelchair access and toilet facilities. Always check this before booking.

Handicapped parking areas, marked with a wheelchair symbol, are widely available, and hefty fines are levied for illegal use of these spaces.

For specialised visitor information in Boston: *tel: (800) 462 5015.*

What to Take

Most people find that they take too much to New England. You can find everything you can get at home and more, and it is all cheaper.

ACKNOWLEDGEMENTS
Thomas Cook Publishing wishes to thank STILLMAN D. ROGERS for the photographs reproduced in this book, to
whom the copyright in the photographs belongs, with the exception of the following:
KAREN BEAULAH 71, 75, 81
TOM BROSS 30a, 30b, 33, 36, 38, 42, 51, 66a, 66b, 67, 159
BILL DESOUSA 85
MASSACHUSETTS OFFICE OF TRAVEL AND TOURISM/KINDRA CLINEFF 78, 144a, 144b

The author would like to thank the following people and institutions for additional help: the state offices of tourism
throughout New England, Maurice and Marjorie Holmes, his wife Bobbie and daughters Emma and Hannah.

Index: MARIE LORIMER
Proofreading: JAN McCANN for CAMBRIDGE PUBLISHING MANAGEMENT LIMITED

Send your thoughts to
books@thomascook.com

We're committed to providing the very best up-to-date information in our travel guides and constantly strive to make them as useful as they can be. You can help us to improve future editions by letting us have your feedback. If you've made a wonderful discovery on your travels that we don't already feature, if you'd like to inform us about recent changes to anything that we do include, or if you simply want to let us know your thoughts about this guidebook and how we can make it even better – we'd love to hear from you.

Send us ideas, discoveries and recommendations today and then look out for your valuable input in the next edition of this title. And, as an extra 'thank you' from Thomas Cook Publishing, you'll be automatically entered into our exciting monthly prize draw.

Emails to the above address, or letters to Travellers Project Editor, Thomas Cook Publishing, PO Box 227, Units 15–16, Coningsby Road, Peterborough PE3 8SB, UK.

Please don't forget to let us know which title your feedback refers to!